ACTS:
THE CHURCH IN ACTION

THE FIERCE STRUGGLE
OF THE CHURCH

VOLUME 4

Acts 15:36–22:1

DR. DAVID JEREMIAH

with Dr. David Jeremiah

CONTENTS

ABOUT
DR. DAVID JEREMIAH
AND TURNING POINT

D r. David Jeremiah is the founder of Turning Point, a ministry committed to providing Christians with sound Bible teaching relevant to today's changing times through radio and television broadcasts, audio series, and books. Dr. Jeremiah's commonsense teaching on topics such as family, prayer, worship, angels, and biblical prophecy forms the foundation of Turning Point.

David and his wife, Donna, reside in El Cajon, California, where he is the senior pastor of Shadow Mountain Community Church and chancellor of San Diego Christian College. David and Donna have four children and nine grandchildren.

In 1982, Dr. Jeremiah brought the same solid teaching to San Diego television that he shares weekly with his congregation. Shortly thereafter, Turning Point expanded its ministry to radio. Dr. Jeremiah's inspiring messages can now be heard worldwide on radio and television.

Because Dr. Jeremiah desires to know his listening audience, he travels nationwide holding "A Night of Encouragement" ministry rallies and Spiritual Enrichment conferences that touch the hearts and lives of many people. According to Dr. Jeremiah, "At some point in time, everyone reaches a turning point; and for every person, that moment is unique, an experience to hold onto forever. There's so much changing in today's world that sometimes it's difficult to choose the right path. Turning Point offers people an understanding of God's Word as well as the opportunity to make a difference in their lives."

Dr. Jeremiah has authored numerous books, including *Escape the Coming Night* (Revelation), *The Handwriting on the Wall* (Daniel), *Overcoming Loneliness, What the Bible Says About Angels, The Joy of Encouragement, Prayer—The Great Adventure, God in You* (Holy Spirit), *Gifts from God* (Parenting), *Jesus' Final Warning, When Your World Falls Apart, Slaying the Giants in Your Life, My Heart's Desire, Sanctuary, Life Wide Open, Searching for Heaven on Earth, The Secret of the Light, Captured by Grace, Discover Paradise, Grace Givers, Why the Nativity,* and *Signs of Life.*

ABOUT THIS STUDY GUIDE

The purpose of this Turning Point study guide is to reinforce Dr. David Jeremiah's dynamic, in-depth teaching, and to aid the reader in applying biblical truth to his or her daily life. This study guide is designed to be used in conjunction with Dr. Jeremiah's *The Church in Action* audio series, but it may also be used by itself for personal or group Bible study.

STRUCTURE OF THE LESSONS

Each lesson is based on one of the messages in *The Church in Action* compact disc series and focuses on specific passages in the Bible. Each lesson is composed of the following elements:

• *Outline*

The outline at the beginning of the lesson gives a clear, concise picture of the passage being studied and provides a helpful framework for readers as they listen to Dr. Jeremiah's teaching.

• *Overview*

The overview summarizes Dr. Jeremiah's teaching on the passage being studied in the lesson. Readers should refer to the Scripture passages in their own Bibles as they study the overview.

• *Application*

This section contains a variety of questions designed to help readers dig deeper into the lesson and the Scriptures, and to apply the lesson to their daily lives. For Bible study groups or Sunday school classes, these questions will provide a springboard for group discussion and interaction.

• *Did You Know?*

This section presents a fascinating fact, historical note, or insight that adds a point of interest to the preceding lesson.

USING THIS GUIDE FOR GROUP STUDY

The lessons in this study guide are suitable for Sunday school classes, small-group studies, elective Bible studies, or home Bible study groups. Each person in the group should have his or her own study guide.

When possible, the study guide should be used with the corresponding compact disc series. You may wish to assign the study guide as homework prior to the meeting of the group and then use the meeting time to listen to the CD and discuss the lesson.

FOR CONTINUING STUDY

A complete catalog of Dr. Jeremiah's materials for personal and group study is available through Turning Point. To obtain a catalog, additional study guides, or more information about Turning Point, call 1-800-947-1993, go online to www.TurningPointOnline.org, or write to: Turning Point, P.O. Box 3838, San Diego, CA 92163.

Dr. Jeremiah's *Turning Point* program is currently heard or viewed around the world on radio, television, and the Internet in English. *Momento Decisivo*, the Spanish translation of Dr. Jeremiah's messages, can be heard on radio in every Spanish speaking country in the world.

Contact Turning Point for radio and television program times and stations in your area. Or visit our website at www.TurningPointOnline.org.

THE CHURCH IN ACTION

VOLUME 4

INTRODUCTION

S omeone has said that wherever the apostle Paul went in his missionary travels the result was either a riot or a revival! In the book of Acts, we can find at least six riots that broke out as a result of his presence and his preaching—and there were also revivals both large and small.

The apostle made four missionary journeys in his lifetime that we know about: three planned and one unplanned. The three planned journeys are recorded in the book of Acts: the first journey in chapters 13–14, the second journey in chapters 15:36–18:22, and the third journey in chapters 18:23–21:16. These three journeys were based out of his "home church" in Antioch of Syria.

Paul had planned a fourth missionary journey that would leave from Jerusalem after he had delivered the relief funds for the Jerusalem church that he had collected from the Macedonian and Greek churches. That journey was to take him from Jerusalem to Rome (where he had never been), and then, using Rome as a launching pad, further west to Spain (Romans 15:24, 28). That's the trip that never happened—at least in the way Paul planned.

He made it to Rome, but as an accused criminal guarded by Roman soldiers. When Paul was arrested in Jerusalem, based on false accusations by the Jews, he eventually appealed to Caesar in Rome—his right as a Roman citizen. His public ministry ended with his arrest in Jerusalem at the end of his third missionary journey—not his ministry, but his public ministry. All the way to Rome, Paul continued to proclaim the grace of God, whether to his Roman guards or the residents of Malta where they were shipwrecked. Even in Caesar's household in Rome, Paul was able to win people to Christ. It was the story of his life—living for the Savior who had rescued him from a life of pride and the yoke of the law.

In this fourth study guide on the book of Acts, we take a slice out of the life of Paul, covering his second and third missionary journeys. We track his travels from Antioch, through Asia Minor, and into Europe where the Gospel is preached for the first time. And then finally to Jerusalem with the relief funds where he is accosted by some of the very Jews who had hounded him and opposed his work in Asia Minor—likely Jews from Ephesus. They were in Jerusalem for the celebration of Pentecost, and are the ones who stirred up Jerusalem and had Paul arrested.

Along the way, those who read closely and devotionally will fall in love with the great apostle of the Gospel of grace—either for the first time or in a renewed way. The apostle Paul is the second most important figure to have played a part on the stage of human history, second only to Jesus Christ himself. And when we follow Paul's path on his journeys, it is not difficult to see why.

Whether causing a riot or a revival, Paul never left any city the same. Whether preaching to the philosophers and intellectuals on Mars Hill in Athens (Acts 17), or leading a humble jailer and his family to Christ in Philippi (Acts 16), Paul was always the same: a humble, sacrificial, servant-leader. It was in his heart and on his bowed back that the Gospel of grace was borne from Jerusalem to as much of the "end of the earth" (Acts 1:8) as he could get to before his time on earth was finished. No one can read the stories of Paul's second and third missionary journeys without being humbled— and challenged to serve Christ in an equally dedicated fashion.

THREE KEYS TO EFFECTIVE MINISTRY

Acts 15:36–16:10

In this lesson we discover three "rights" necessary for effective ministry.

OUTLINE

Look around Christendom today and you will observe an endless array of ministries and methods for carrying out the spread of the Gospel. In spite of the wealth of our resources and reasons, today's church would do well to recall the focused simplicity of the early church's priorities.

I. **Ministry Key Number One: The Right Purpose**
   A. The Purpose of Edification
   B. The Purpose of Encouragement
   C. The Purpose of Evangelism

II. **Ministry Key Number Two: The Right People**
   A. The Selection of Silas
   B. The Selection of Timothy

III. **Ministry Key Number Three: The Right Place**
   A. The Divine Denial
   B. The Divine Direction

I t's easy to read the history of the early church in the book of
Acts and marvel at its accomplishments. They had few of the
material and technological resources we have today, yet they
seemed to have made rapid strides toward fulfilling the Great
Commission in their day.

This illustration is apropos to the early church's accomplishments: Think of a river that is very narrow and fast-flowing at its
source but very wide and slow-moving hundreds of miles down-
stream. The narrow banks near the mouth of the river keep it focused
and force the water to flow quickly. But as the river leaves the
mountainous headwaters behind and flattens out on the plains,
the breadth allowed by the wide banks causes it to slow down
and meander instead of rushing forward with force. Power and
focus are replaced by breadth and loss of influence.

Sometimes that happens in ministry—we start strong and
gradually lose the power we once had. And that may have happened to the church of Jesus Christ. It will be helpful for us to
review what made the early church so powerful and helped it
change the world so rapidly.

MINISTRY KEY NUMBER ONE:
THE RIGHT PURPOSE (15:36, 41; 16:4–5)

Keeping our focus in ministry depends on understanding the
purposes of all Christian ministry: edification, encouragement,
and evangelism.

The Purpose of Edification (15:36, 41)

In verse 36 we find Paul expressing the need to return to the
churches he and Barnabas started to "see how they [were] doing."
It was not Paul's heart to win people to Christ and then allow
them to struggle on their own. He was a spiritual pediatrician as
well as an obstetrician! He wanted to return and make sure the
new believers they had left behind were growing in the Lord and
being built up in their faith.

In verse 41 we find Paul and Barnabas doing just that: "And
he went through Syria and Cilicia, strengthening the churches."
And in 16:5, "So the churches were strengthened in the faith . . . ."
"Strengthened" is a medical term, often used to refer to the healing
of a lame person (Acts 3:7, 16). So edification is the process of

strengthening those who are weak, building them up in the faith. The need for edification is permanent—a focus of the early and the modern church.

The Purpose of Encouragement (16:4)

A problem arose in the early church over how Jewish and Gentile believers should relate to one another. A conference was held in Jerusalem to resolve the problem (Acts 15); and in 16:4, we find Paul and Barnabas delivering to the churches they had founded "the decrees to keep, which were determined by the apostles and elders at Jerusalem." In Paul and Barnabas's absence, false teachers had tried to mislead the new believers; and it was Paul's desire to encourage them with the truth: All that was necessary to be saved was faith in the Lord Jesus Christ. They were free from laboring under the demands of the law as a means for acceptance by God.

The Purpose of Evangelism (16:5b)

As Paul and Barnabas edified and encouraged the new believers, the third purpose of the church was accomplished: "So the churches . . . increased in number daily" (16:5b). New converts were added to the churches on a daily basis as they saw the results of knowing Christ in the lives of the believers.

This is the fourth "report" of the numerical growth of the church given in Acts (see 6:7; 9:31; 12:24 for the first three). All living things, if they are healthy, should experience growth—and the church is no exception. Individual churches may experience barriers to growth such as facility size or geographical or demographic factors. But those barriers should be overcome so that growth continues. Growth is at the heart of Christ's Great Commission (Matthew 28:19–20).

The danger with edification and encouragement is that we can grow content and comfortable—we can stop welcoming new people into our midst who don't know Christ. We can resist dealing with the immaturity of unsaved people or new believers. And that's when growth stagnates. But the purpose of edification and encouragement is to make us mature enough to stay focused on the third purpose of the church.

MINISTRY KEY NUMBER TWO: THE RIGHT PEOPLE (15:37–40)

In his book *Good to Great—Why Some Companies Make the Leap . . . and Others Don't*, author Jim Collins reports the findings of a study of 11,000 companies. One of his findings was this: "Get the right people on the bus and get the wrong people off the bus, and then decide where the bus is going."[1]

Paul and Barnabas made lots of "personnel" decisions in their missionary activity in order to stay focused on accomplishing the purposes of the church.

The Selection of Silas (15:37–40)

Barnabas wanted to take John Mark with them on their journey to revisit the churches, but Paul refused since Mark had abandoned them on their first journey (Acts 13:13). So Barnabas took Mark and went to Cyprus, and Paul chose Silas to accompany him through Syria and Cilicia.

Barnabas was called "Son of Encouragement" in the early church (Acts 4:36) because he was such a people person. Paul, however, was goal-oriented, not allowing any person to stand in the way of accomplishing the mission. And both are necessary.

In this instance, Paul put John Mark "off the bus" and invited Silas to climb aboard for the journey. Silas became Paul's partner in ministry and a faithful one at that. In Acts 16 we find him enduring incarceration with Paul in the jail in Philippi. It seems Paul made the right decision in this case by replacing John Mark with Silas. Personnel decisions are not always easy, but they are always necessary.

The Selection of Timothy (16:1–3)

When Paul and Silas arrived in Derbe and Lystra, they met a young convert named Timothy who was well spoken of by the church.

1. The Character of Timothy (16:1–2)

Timothy's mother was a Jewish convert to Christ while his father was a (apparently unconverted) Gentile. It may be that Timothy and his mother were converted when Paul came through the region on his first missionary journey. Timothy soon became like a spiritual son to Paul (1 Timothy 1:2a, 18; 2 Timothy 1:2; 2:1). He had made great spiritual progress which really caught Paul's eye. Even though Paul had been stoned on his first trip through Lystra (Acts 14:19), something good had come from it: Timothy. Just as Paul was probably touched by the stoning of Stephen (Acts 7:59–8:1a), so had Timothy perhaps been touched by the stoning of Paul in Lystra.

Timothy means "dear to God" and not only was Timothy dear to God, he became dear to Paul as well. In spite of coming from a mixed marriage (ethnically and spiritually), Timothy was influenced by his godly Jewish mother. Both his grandmother and his mother had become believers in Christ (2 Timothy 1:5), and they exerted a strong influence on Timothy. They taught Timothy the Jewish Scriptures and helped him grow in his relationship with Jesus. Even the people in Iconium, 18 miles from Lystra, had heard of Timothy and respected him (Acts 16:2). Paul perhaps saw Timothy as a worthy young replacement for the undependable John Mark. He became Paul's most trusted young protégé.

Timothy is the only person in the New Testament that Paul addressed as "man of God" (1 Timothy 6:11)—no small commendation for Timothy's character.

2. The Circumcision of Timothy (16:3)

It was clear from the decisions of the church leaders in Jerusalem that no believer in Christ had to submit to Jewish circumcision (Acts 15:5 ff.). Yet before leaving Lystra, Paul circumcised Timothy "because of the Jews who were in that region, for they all knew that [Timothy's] father was Greek."

It's clear that Paul didn't circumcise Timothy for salvific reasons. As the son of a Jewish mother, Timothy would be regarded as a Jew by the Jews to whom Paul would preach as they continued their journey. If Timothy were uncircumcised, it would be a stumbling block to the Jews. So to remove that obstacle, Paul circumcised Timothy so the unsaved Jews would have no ceremonial reasons to reject Paul and Timothy and their preaching. By being circumcised, Timothy could not be accused of being only "half-Jewish" since his father was a Gentile.

In 1 Corinthians 9:19–22, Paul established the principle of doing what is necessary to remove obstacles to people's faith: "I have become all things to all men, that I might by all means save some" (verse 22b). He would make no concessions or compromises when it came to the truth. But cultural and ceremonial issues were different. Paul was willing to be accommodating in order that the Gospel might be received.

Paul didn't flaunt his liberty in the face of those who were bound by the law. He was sensitive and humble, knowing that unsaved people were without spiritual understanding. So he extended as much grace as possible to them—an example being, asking Timothy to be circumcised for the sake of the Gospel.

MINISTRY KEY NUMBER THREE: THE RIGHT PLACE (16:6–10)

The third key to ministry as demonstrated by Paul is being in the right place—the place where God puts you.

The Divine Denial (16:6–8)

Paul and his companions attempted to go east toward Asia with the Gospel, but "they were forbidden by the Holy Spirit" (verse 6). They then turned toward Bithynia but "the Spirit did not permit them" (verse 7). So they were "0 for 2" in terms of finding God's place for them to minister.

We aren't told how the Spirit directed Paul's group, but I personally wonder if it might have been illness since it was about this time that Luke, the physician, joined them. In verse 10 we find Luke using the pronoun "we" for the first time, Luke being the author of Acts (Acts 1:1).

Whatever the reason, Paul was told "No" by God twice when it came to the right place to minister.

The Divine Direction (16:9–10)

Denial was to be replaced by direction as Paul had a vision from the Lord: A man from Macedonia appeared to Paul, asking the apostle to come over and "help us" (verse 9). Paul concluded that the Lord had called them to preach the Gospel to the Macedonians. In other words, instead of Asia, God was directing Paul to leave Asia Minor and go into Europe.

Paul was sensitive enough to the Spirit of God that he could tell the difference between "No" and "Yes" when it came to discerning God's will. And he was obedient enough to respond to both: After he had seen the vision, Paul and his companions "immediately" went into Macedonia (verse 10)—not eventually, but immediately.

So the three keys to ministry revolve around purpose, people, and place.

- Purpose is three-fold: edification, encouragement, and evangelism.
- People: If you have the right people (of God's choosing) on your team, ministry is a joy. If there are people on that team who shouldn't be there, trying to manage the people problems that result can sap all your spiritual energy.

- Place: Ultimately, if you aren't where God wants you to be in ministry, you will have little success. There are plenty of people who will give you advice about where you should be serving. But everything you are told by other people must be confirmed by God's direction and leading.

Too often Christians think that a need constitutes a call. Paul was blocked from going to two different regions where there was definitely a need: Asia and Bithynia. But neither was the place where God wanted Paul to serve, so he was blocked from going there. Your awareness of a long-term need is not necessarily the confirmation you need to meet that need. (That is not to say we shouldn't be available to serve the Lord and others when called upon, but we should confirm long-term service commitments with Him.) The only way to be able to say "Yes" to the place God wants you to serve is if you say "No" to the places that are not His will for you.

G. Campbell Morgan was a great preacher of a former generation. Summarizing these lessons from Paul's experience, he wrote, "Oh, to go, not where I may choose, even by my love of the Lord, but where I am driven by the Lord's command. Circumstances of difficulty are opportunities for faith, and the measure of our perplexity in service and in Christian life is the measure of our opportunity. . . . It is better to go to Troas with God, than anywhere else without Him."

To those words, I say, "Amen!" When God calls you to serve, make sure you serve for the right purpose. Make sure you get the right people. By all means, get in the right place. And whatever God tells you to do, do it immediately.

Note:

1. Jim Collins, *Good to Great: Why Some Companies Make the Leap . . . and Others Don't* (New York: HarperCollins, 2001).

APPLICATION

1. Based on the following references in Acts, note the ways that the church grew after the pouring out of the Spirit at Pentecost:

   a. How many were saved at Pentecost? (2:42)

   b. What continued to happen after Pentecost? (2:47)

   c. How large did the church become under Peter and John's ministry in Jerusalem? (4:4)

   d. What impact did the apostles' miracles have on the growth of the church? (5:12–14)

   e. What manifestation of growth is recorded in 6:1–2?

   f. What surprising category of people in Jerusalem began to turn to the Lord? (6:7)

   g. What opportunity does "peace" allow for? (9:31)

h. What caused two entire towns to turn to Christ? (9:32–35)

i. What happened in Joppa that caused many to believe? (9:40–43)

j. What must be present for people to turn to the Lord? (11:21)

k. What impact did the fullness of the Spirit have on evangelism in Antioch? (11:24)

l. What activity is essential to evangelism as evidenced in Derbe? (14:21)

m. What is the evidence of "strength" (maturity)? (16:5)

n. What effect does "examining the Word" have on evangelism? (17:11–12)

o. If you could implement one strategy at your church in order to help it grow, what would it be and why?

2. What relationship was John Mark to Barnabas? (Colossians 4:10)

a. What evidence is there that John Mark and Paul were ultimately reconciled in Christ? (2 Timothy 4:11)

b. How should Christians handle disagreements in personal or personnel matters so as not to cause offense?

3. What do you find in Philippians 2:19–22 that reveals Paul's feelings about his protégé Timothy?

DID YOU KNOW?

The apostolic council of church leaders held in Jerusalem (Acts 15) was the first of many that have been held since. The first eight church councils were ecumenical in scope, including representatives from across the breadth of Christendom (all dates are A.D.): the First Council of Nicaea (325), the First Council of Constantinople (381), the First Council of Ephesus (431), the Second Council of Ephesus (449), the Council of Chalcedon (451), the Second Council of Constantinople (553), the Third Council of Constantinople (680–681), and the Second Council of Nicaea (787). One of the primary purposes of these councils was to refute heretical teachings and establish orthodox doctrine.

EUROPE'S FIRST CHRISTIANS

Acts 16:11–19

*In this lesson we meet the first two recipients
of the Christian Gospel in Europe.*

OUTLINE

In America it is hard to keep in mind that the gospel of Christ arose
in an Oriental (Middle Eastern) culture instead of an Occidental
(Western) culture. Eventually, all of Europe became Christian
as a result of Paul's crossing the Aegean Sea from Asia Minor with
the Gospel.

I. **The Salvation of a Sophisticated Woman**
   A. Lydia's City
   B. Lydia's Custom
   C. Lydia's Conversion
   D. Lydia's Confession

II. **The Salvation of a Slave Girl**
   A. She Was Demon Possessed
   B. She Was Dangerous to the Gospel
   C. She Was Dramatically Saved
   D. She Was Delivered from Demon Control

There have been many famous ocean voyages recorded in human history—the sailing of Leif Ericsson's ships to what is now the northern reaches of North America around A.D. 1000, the westward voyages of Columbus in the late 1400s, the circumnavigation of the globe by Magellan's ships in the 1520s, the sailing of the Mayflower to America in 1620 to name a few. But none are as important as a voyage that left Troas in Asia Minor in A.D. 59 and landed in Neapolis in Macedonia (today's Europe).

On that voyage were the apostle Paul, his coworker Silas, Luke the physician, and Paul's protégé, Timothy. The reason this voyage was so important was that it introduced the Christian Gospel to Europe. In terms of the development of Western (European) Civilization, of which America is a by-product, no journey comes close in importance.

This voyage was a continuation of Paul's second missionary journey (A.D. 49–52). It began in Antioch and headed west into Asia Minor where Paul revisited churches that were established on his first missionary journey. In Troas on the seacoast, Paul had a vision of a man in Macedonia calling him to "come over and help us" (Acts 16:9). Since the Holy Spirit had previously prevented Paul's party from going into Asia and Bithynia, Paul concluded the vision was God's direction. And so the Gospel crossed the Asia-Europe boundary, and the history of the world was changed. God is in charge of not only the *steps,* but the *stops* of a righteous man.

Crossing into Europe, Paul made his way to the city of Philippi, the foremost city of that part of Macedonia. Acts 16:11–19 describes Paul's entry into Philippi and sets the stage for the dramatic events that were to follow.

THE SALVATION OF A SOPHISTICATED WOMAN (16:11–15)

The first European (mentioned in Scripture) to become a Christian was a woman named Lydia.

Lydia's City (16:11–12)

The term "straight course" in verse 11 is a nautical term that means they were sailing with the wind—they had the wind at their back as they sailed from Troas to Samothrace and then to Neapolis, the port city of Philippi. I like the spiritual image suggested by that term: When we are obeying the will of God, we have the wind of the Spirit aiding us as we go. It doesn't mean life will always be smooth sailing, as Paul would later discover when he was shipwrecked on the way to Rome. But it does mean God is with us in our journey when we travel in His will.

Philippi was a Roman colony, taking its name in 356 B.C. from Philip II of Macedon, the father of Alexander the Great. Philippi was a favored city of Rome, as a great victory in the second Roman civil war was won there in 42 B.C. The citizens of Philippi were exempt from provincial Roman taxes. The city was a crown jewel in the Roman system, benefiting from the favor of Rome in ways other cities did not. Since Paul seemed to prefer to establish a beachhead for ministry in a key city of a region, we shouldn't be surprised that he picked Philippi.

Lydia's Custom (16:13)

Because there were relatively few Jews living in Philippi, there was no synagogue. (Rabbinic tradition stated that at least ten Jewish men were needed in order to form a synagogue.) Paul couldn't follow his normal practice of going first to the synagogue (Acts 17:1, 10, 17; 18:4), so he went where the Jews met to pray on the Sabbath: by the side of the local river.

The group meeting by the river on that Sabbath was made up of women, so Paul and his coworkers joined them. Jewish men had a history of thanking God that they were neither "Gentile nor slave nor a woman." So for a Jewish teacher to be willing to sit down with a group of women and speak with them would have immediately impressed the women that day. The Macedonian in Paul's vision was a man, but the first people he encountered who were open to the Gospel were women!

Lydia's Conversion (16:14)

One of the women was Lydia, "a seller of purple from the city of Thyatira, who worshipped God." Lydia was a Gentile, not a Jewess; a Jewish proselyte, or "God-fearer," like Cornelius (Acts 10:2). She wanted to know God, but all she knew was what she had learned from Jewish tradition. She was a businesswoman—a seller of dyed purple cloth. She probably imported the cloth from Thyatira and resold it in Philippi. Purple was the color of royalty and nobility, so she probably was very successful. We know she had a home large enough to host Paul and his team (Acts 16:15, 40).

We can see three things about Lydia that made her ready to receive the gospel of Christ.

1. She Was a Worshipper of God

Lydia worshipped God as best she knew how. Like a lot of people, Lydia wanted to know God but just needed someone to tell her how.

2. She Was a Listener

When it became clear that the strangers who joined the women were speaking something new, Lydia could have left. But she didn't. She was hungry, and so she listened to Paul's teaching.

3. She Had a Tender Heart

Verse 14 says, "The Lord opened her heart to heed the things spoken by Paul." This was clearly a divine appointment as the Lord brought a seeker and a preacher together. Only God can open a person's heart to the Gospel. Our job is to present the Gospel clearly and persuasively and leave the results to God.

Lydia's ears, eyes, and heart were opened to Paul and his Gospel message, and she believed on Jesus Christ and was saved.

Lydia's Confession (16:15)

After Lydia placed her faith in Christ, "she and her household were baptized."

1. Her Obedient Heart (16:15a)

The biblical pattern is clear: Salvation is followed (usually immediately) by baptism. We see this consistently throughout the book of Acts. Though baptism plays no part in our salvation, it is an outward evidence of an inner transformation that has taken place. There is no reason for salvation not to be followed by baptism.

The reference to her "household" doesn't mean that they were automatically saved because Lydia was saved. It means that the impact of her conversion was so strong that those over whom Lydia exercised influence were likewise convinced of the truth of the Gospel and believed and were baptized. It probably included her immediate family and her extended family as well, including household servants. The conversion of Lydia and her family drove a stake deep into the spiritual soil of Europe.

2. Her Open Home (16:15b)

Not only did Lydia open her heart to the Lord, she opened her home to Paul and his companions. It appears from verse 40 that Lydia's house became their base of operations while they were in

Philippi. Lydia's faith was immediately manifested in the good work of hospitality.

Lydia was like a lot of people: well-intentioned, moral, but lost. That was true of the Ethiopian official (Acts 8), the apostle Paul (Saul of Tarsus) (Acts 9), and Cornelius, the Roman centurion (Acts 10). And I fear it is true of many people who fill the pews in churches today, people who believe their respect for God, their financial offerings, and their good works will win them a place in heaven. Unfortunately, the only way to be saved is the way Lydia was saved—by opening one's heart to the gospel of Jesus Christ.

As you read Lydia's story, make sure you don't miss the most important point: Paul didn't baptize her because she was a God-fearer. She was baptized because of her conversion, her personal faith in Jesus Christ as her Savior from sin. If you have never placed your faith in Christ the way Lydia did, now would be a good time to do so.

THE SALVATION OF A SLAVE GIRL (16:16–19)

The second European to be saved was also a woman— a demonized slave girl.

She Was Demon Possessed (16:16)

There is always opposition to the Gospel, and in Philippi it came first from a demonized young woman who brought her own-ers income by telling people's fortunes. She was like Simon the sorcerer in Samaria (Acts 8) and Bar-Jesus in Paphos (Acts 13)— individuals used by Satan to hinder the spread of the Gospel.

In the Greek, the "spirit of divination" is literally "a spirit of Python," Python being the snake that guarded the famous oracle at Delphi in Greek mythology. Python was killed by Apollo, the god of prophecy, so "python" came to be associated with anyone who told the future. In our day we would refer to her as a medium or a fortune-teller. Her owners profited greatly from her association with evil spirits.

In his commentary on Acts, Pastor Kent Hughes has written, "The poor girl was 'demonized,' filled with a demon or demons who revealed the future to her clients. She was a clairvoyant owned by spiritual pimps who sold her metaphysical powers. Satan's strategy was obvious: to derail the Gospel by infiltrating it, by forming an apparent alliance with Christ's work—for his own ends, of course. He loves to distort the Gospel just enough to twist it into a deadly heresy." [1]

She Was Dangerous to the Gospel *(16:17–18a)*

The girl followed Paul's band around proclaiming, "These men are the servants of the Most High God, who proclaim to us the way of salvation. And this she did for many days." This seems odd given that she was a tool of Satan. (See a similar oddity in Mark 1:24–26.)

The reason Paul wanted nothing to do with her, in spite of her message, was because she was well known in Philippi as a fortune-teller. People were aware of her connection to Roman mythology and dark spirits, and Paul wanted nothing like that to be associated with the Gospel. She was in the same category as the demons referred to in James 2:19: "Even the demons believe—and tremble!" Just because a demonized person says something true about God doesn't mean they believe it in a God-honoring way.

If Paul had allowed this girl's charade to continue, it would have made the Gospel appear to be just another synchronistic religious blend so common in that day. Plus, it would have made it appear that she was part of Paul's group of workers, something Paul could not allow to happen. She was a danger to the progress of the Gospel and had to be dealt with.

She Was Dramatically Saved *(16:18b)*

Luke tells us that Paul had finally had enough—he was "greatly annoyed" after "many days" of this girl's intrusions into their work. So Paul spoke—not to the girl, but to the spirit in the girl—and commanded the spirit to "come out of her. And he came out that very hour."

As soon as the name of Christ was spoken, the demon fled; and the girl was set free from her bondage. The words of Charles Wesley's hymn, "O For a Thousand Tongues to Sing," are descriptive of that moment:

He breaks the pow'r of cancelled sin,
    He sets the prisoner free;
    His blood can make the foulest clean;
    His blood availed for me.

She Was Delivered from Demon Control *(16:19–22)*

Because the girl had lost the source of her fortune-telling ability, her owners were furious. Paul had ruined their lucrative source of income, and they dragged Paul and Silas "into the marketplace to the authorities." In the next lesson, we will get into the details of what happened to these two. In short, the authorities sided with the businessmen whose source of income had been taken away: Paul and Silas were stripped, beaten severely, and thrown into jail. But the power of God would soon be displayed even more dramatically than it was in the deliverance of the slave girl.

We will find in Acts 16 that three objects of Jewish enmity all came to Christ: a woman, a slave girl, and a Gentile (jailer). Luke wants the record to show that, with God, there is no male or female, slave or free, Greek or Jew (Galatians 3:28). All are one in Christ Jesus. In spite of the trouble he encountered in Philippi, the church there became Paul's favorite.

Ten years after starting the church in Philippi, he wrote tenderly to them from prison in the letter we know as the book of Philippians. The church had ministered to him with gifts for his support while he was in prison, and he expressed his gratitude to them (Philippians 4:10–20).

You may come to identify with one of the people in Acts 16 who found new life in Christ: a sophisticated businessperson, a girl with a dark past, or a wage-earner making a living for his family. You can find the same freedom in Christ, by faith, that they did.

Note:
1. R. Kent Hughes, *Acts: The Church Afire* (Wheaton: Crossway Books, 1996), 214.

APPLICATION

1. Review the events recorded in Acts 13:13–48.

   a. What was (part of) the synagogue practice? (verse 15a)

   b. What invitation was extended to Paul and his companions? (verse 15b)

   c. What two categories of people were present in the synagogue meeting? (verses 16, 26)

   d. What was Paul's purpose in delivering such a long "exhortation"? (verses 23, 38–39)

   e. How did Paul's scholarly, rabbinic training help him in placing Jesus in the context of Israel's history?

   f. What was the immediate reaction of many in the synagogue? (verses 42–43)

   g. After a week to consider what Paul had taught, what was the response of some of the Jews? (verse 45)

h. Compare Paul's words in Romans 1:16 with his words in verses 46–47.

i. Assuming Paul spoke similar words to Lydia and her companions in Philippi, how does verse 48 provide insight into how Lydia probably responded?

2. Read Mark 1:21–28.

    a. Where was Jesus on this occasion, and what was He doing? (verse 21)

    b. How was the condition of the man in verse 24 similar to the girl Paul encountered in Philippi? (Acts 16:16–17)

    c. Describe the antagonistic things the spirit said through the man. (verse 24)

    d. What did the spirit say about Jesus that was true? (verse 24)

    e. To whom do the two different "him's" refer in verse 25? To whom was Jesus talking?

f. What can you conclude about evil spirits from this and the instance in Philippi—about their knowledge?

g. How was Paul's response parallel to Jesus' response?

h. Why is saying things that are true not enough reason to support a person's claims?

3. How did Paul make reference to his meeting with Lydia and her friends in Philippians 1:5?

DID YOU KNOW?

Up until the time of the Babylonian exile, the formal religious life of Israel centered around the temple. Scholars believe that once Israel was removed from Jerusalem and the temple and deported to Babylon, the need for continuing religious instruction gave rise to the synagogue—a place not for worship (that priority was reserved for a one-day-restored temple) but for religious instruction. Even when many Jews returned to the homeland, many remained dispersed; and synagogues multiplied wherever Jews settled. It was to these places of Jewish religious instruction outside Israel's homeland that Paul took the Gospel when he entered cities in the Roman Empire.

JAIL BREAK

Acts 16:19–40

In this lesson we discover the essence of the Christian gospel.

OUTLINE

If you were asked by a dying person how to be saved—how to know God and experience the forgiveness of sins—what would you say? When the apostle Paul was asked that question by a man who feared for his life, he responded with the simplest statement of the Gospel in the Bible.

I. **The Arrest of Paul and Silas**

II. **The Accusations Against Paul and Silas**
   A. The Ethnic Charge
   B. The Civil Charge
   C. The Religious Charge

III. **The Action Taken Against Paul and Silas**
   A. They Were Indicted
   B. They Were Imprisoned

IV. **The Attitude of Paul and Silas**

V. **The Advantage of Paul and Silas**
   A. Their Impact on the Prison
   B. Their Impact on the Prisoners
   C. Their Impact on the Prison Keeper

VI. **The Assertion of Paul and Silas**

W e have a lot to cover in this lesson regarding Paul and Silas's experience in jail, so let's review briefly how they got there.

Responding to a vision from the Lord, Paul and his companions left Asia Minor and entered Europe, heading for the city of Philippi—the crown jewel of the Roman region. After winning a small group of converts, Paul set about preaching. When he cast a demon out of a slave girl who was used as a fortune-teller by her owners, the owners lost the income the girl provided them. As a result, the owners dragged Paul and Silas before the magistrates who had them beaten and thrown in jail.

In this lesson we will see God's miraculous deliverance of His two preachers and the conversion of yet more Philippians to Christ as a result (Acts 16:19–40).

The Arrest of Paul and Silas (16:19)

As soon as a person's money is touched, his or her true character is revealed. The evil men who used a demon-possessed slave girl to bring them profit turned on Paul and Silas for having interfered in their lucrative work. And as so often happens, the officials who should have been prosecuting the businessmen for their abuse of the young girl prosecuted those who were standing up for righteousness and justice. Even today we see the laws of the land protecting and thereby sustaining pornography, perversions, abortions, and other unrighteous activity.

The Accusations Against Paul and Silas (16:20–21)

Just as the charges brought against Jesus were trumped up and spurious, so were the charges brought against Paul and Silas.

The Ethnic Charge (16:20)

They were first accused of "being Jews." Timothy and Luke, Paul's other two companions, being Gentiles, were not arrested. There is clearly an ethnic, or racial, bias on the part of Paul and Silas's accusers. But the men had it wrong: Silas was a Roman citizen (verses 37–38) and likely a Gentile, a proselyte to the Jewish religion before becoming a Christian.

There were so few Jews in Philippi that it was easy to suggest that Paul and Barnabas, as Jews, were attempting to stir up the city.

The Civil Charge (16:20)

The civil charge was that Paul and Silas had "exceedingly [troubled the] city" of Philippi. Roman colonies like Philippi were intended to be models of peace—disruptions were not tolerated. So it was easy to get the magistrates' attention with charges of troubling the city—that is, causing a riot (Greek *ektarasso*).

The Religious Charge (16:21)

The final charge was that Paul and Silas were teaching customs "which are not lawful for us, being Romans, to receive or observe." The problem with this charge is that there is no evidence that anyone in Paul's party had taught anyone except Jews and Jewish proselytes like Lydia. But these men were determined to see Paul and Silas punished, so they made up these charges along with the others.

THE ACTION TAKEN AGAINST PAUL AND SILAS (16:22–24)

Though they were falsely accused, Paul and Silas were severely punished.

They Were Indicted (16:22)

What started as false accusations by a few men quickly turned into a mob that was intent on seeing Paul and Silas punished: A "multitude rose up together against them." The magistrates joined the mob, tearing off Paul's and Silas's clothing and ordering them to be "beaten with rods."

This is one of the three times Paul was "beaten with rods" to which he refers in 2 Corinthians 11:25. The beating seems to have been an impulsive act on the part of the magistrates—the real punishment was yet to come.

They Were Imprisoned (16:23–24)

The jailer was commanded to keep Paul and Silas securely so he "fastened their feet in the stocks" within the jail (verse 24). Stocks were not just for security purposes. They were an additional form of punishment: a square log split in two with holes drilled for the prisoner's ankles. The top half of the log was removed, the prisoner's ankles were positioned in the bottom half of the ankle holes, then the top half of the log was laid down on top of the ankles and fastened. The prisoner might be left in this position for days, seated, and unable to move his legs at all.

So Paul and Silas were stripped, beaten, locked in the stocks in the interior of the jail, and left to suffer in this terrible place—all for telling others about Jesus.

The Attitude of
Paul and Silas (16:25)

Paul and Silas might have felt sorry for themselves, wondering why God called them to Macedonia only to be beaten and thrown in jail. Not so! At midnight Paul and Silas were entertaining the other prisoners with songs of praise to God. Notice: hymns *to* God, not hymns *about* God. They were not mad at God over what had happened. Indeed, they were praising Him in the midst of their circumstances.

Kent Hughes has written, "Paul and his Gospel companions sang because they knew God had called them across the expanse of Asia Minor. They sang because they believed rightly that they were prisoners of Christ and not of Rome." [1] Paul would later write to the Philippians that it is "granted" to Christians "not only to believe in [Christ], but also to suffer for His sake" (Philippians 1:29). That is, suffering for the Gospel is a privilege granted by God.

In Acts 12, we saw Peter in jail; and he was sleeping soundly while chained to Roman guards. And here Paul and Silas were singing praises to God. These Christian men's attitude in the face of suffering surely spoke volumes to those who observed them. They were at peace while in the midst of a painful situation.

The Advantage of
Paul and Silas (16:26–34)

Those in jail with Paul and Silas quickly discovered there was an advantage to having them there.

Their Impact on the Prison (16:26)

Around midnight, there was "a great earthquake" in Philippi—the doors to the prison were opened and "everyone's chains were loosed."

Their Impact on the Prisoners (16:28)

It would be natural for prisoners to flee a jail when their chains have fallen off and the doors have been flung open. But Paul called to the jailer and said, "Do yourself no harm, for we are all here." The jailer likely feared for his life, thinking that all the prisoners had fled—and he had been told to keep Paul and Silas secure. Why the prisoners didn't flee, we aren't told. There must have been something so spellbinding about Paul and Silas that it just captivated the other prisoners. Their carnal urge to flee and protect themselves went dormant in the presence of praises to God.

Their Impact on the Prison Keeper (16:27, 29–34)

The impact on the prison keeper constitutes the rest of the story. He received a miracle even greater than the miracle of Paul and Silas's release from prison.

1. Safety (16:27)

A Roman prison guard was required to suffer whatever punishment his prisoners were destined to suffer if they escaped. In this case, Paul and Silas saved the guard's life by remaining in the jail after the earthquake freed them. He was about to kill himself rather than be killed by the authorities.

2. Salvation (16:29–31)

The guard was saved physically, but he was also saved spiritually.

a. His Whole Heart (16:29–31a)

The guard asked, "What must I do to be saved?" But he wasn't talking about being saved physically since the prisoners were still there, and he wasn't in danger of losing his life. No, he wanted what Paul and Silas had and was asking how to get it. And the answer was simple—for him and for you and me: "Believe on the Lord Jesus Christ, and you will be saved" (verse 31).

b. His Whole Household (16:31–34)

The second half of verse 31 says, "You [will be saved], you and your household." Paul baptized the jailer and all his household—and some Christian groups today practice infant baptism on the basis of this verse. Let's review what happened in this situation in chronological order:

(1) The Promise of Salvation to His Whole Household

Paul made the promise to the jailer that he and his "whole household" would be saved if they "[believed] on the Lord Jesus Christ."

(2) The Preaching of Salvation to His Whole Household

Paul then "spoke the word of the Lord to him and to all who were in his house" (verse 32). So the promise and the preaching were both directed to the "whole household."

(3) The Acceptance of Salvation by His Whole Household

The acceptance of salvation was also by the whole household: "Having believed in God with all his household" (verse 34b). They all received the Gospel and they all believed.

(4) The Proof of Salvation by His Whole Household

As a result of all the household believing, they were all baptized: "And immediately he and all his family were baptized" (verse 33).

Therefore, infant baptism is not taught or even suggested in these verses. The only reason the whole household was baptized is that the whole household believed the Gospel. Only believers in Christ were baptized that night in Philippi. Therefore, it was believer's baptism, not infant baptism, that this passage teaches. Besides, the text nowhere says that there were infants in this household. The clear implication is that all the members of the household were old enough to believe the Gospel. [Note: This is one of several instances in Acts where baptism follows immediately on the heels of belief.]

3. Service (16:33–34)

The jailer immediately put his newfound faith into action by caring for Paul and Silas—washing their wounds and feeding them a meal. It must have been a celebratory atmosphere since the text says that the jailer "rejoiced, having believed in God with all his household" (verse 34). It's no wonder that joy in the Lord became the theme of Paul's letter to the Philippians. Paul wrote that letter while in a different prison years after this event, but his letter no doubt reminded the Philippians of the joy that came out of his jail experience in Philippi.

THE ASSERTION OF PAUL AND SILAS (16:35–40)

Paul and Silas were still officially prisoners even though they had been taken into the jailer's home for food and medical attention. But the day after they had been imprisoned, the magistrates apparently had changed their minds about incarcerating Paul and Silas. Perhaps the combination of the earthquake, plus the fact that the charges were baseless to begin with, made them decide they wanted nothing to do with those two. And so they ordered Paul and Silas released.

But Paul and Silas refused to go. Their rights as Roman citizens had been violated as they had been beaten and imprisoned without the due process of Roman law. Not only was that illegal, it was illegal for a Roman citizen to be expelled from a Roman city. So Paul stood his ground. And the magistrates suddenly feared for their own livelihoods. If word got back to higher officials in Rome that the magistrates had violated the rights of Roman citizens, they themselves would be guilty and be punished.

Paul wasn't just being obstinate. He was trying to establish the fact, for the future good of the Philippian church, that Christianity was not against Roman law. By the magistrates' releasing them publicly, admitting they had been wrong, the church would be protected from future harassment. As a Roman citizen, Paul knew the law and knew how to use it to protect the church that would be left behind. The magistrates met Paul's request and "asked them" (not "demanded") that they leave Philippi.

If there is one lesson to take away from this marvelous story of salvation in the Philippian jail, it is this: the simplicity of the Gospel. Question: "What must I do to be saved?" Answer: "Believe on the Lord Jesus Christ and you will be saved." (Acts 16:31) Perhaps if we communicated the Gospel as simply and clearly as did the early church, more people would be saved.

Bishop John Taylor Smith was the chaplain general of the British Army during World War I. He gave all military chaplain candidates a simple test to determine their adequacy to serve as military chaplains. He asked them to explain what they would tell a dying soldier about salvation who only had three minutes to live. If they could not communicate the Gospel simply and clearly in that brief time, they were disqualified and not allowed to serve as chaplains.[2]

There are Christian leaders today who would fail that test because they have blended "churchianity" with "Christianity." They have allowed peripheral issues to become part of the salvation message and led people astray in the process. I trust this lesson has clarified for you the essence of the Gospel message as it did for the Philippian jailer—and that you have believed on the Lord Jesus Christ and been saved.

Notes:

1. R. Kent Hughes, *Acts: The Church Afire* (Wheaton: Crossway Books, 1996), 217.

2. J. Wilbur Chapman, "The Minister's Handicap," (American Tract Society, 1918), Quoted by R. Kent Hughes, *Acts: The Church Afire* (Wheaton: Crossway Books, 1996), 218.

APPLICATION

1. What is the requirement for salvation found in Mark 16:16?

    a. How is this different from Acts 16:31?

    b. Read Matthew 28:19–20 and explain how it helps to reconcile the verses in Mark and Acts.

    c. What is the formula for salvation found in Romans 10:9?

    d. In light of Matthew 10:32, is "confession" actually a second requirement for salvation beyond faith? Why or why not?

    e. What does confessing Christ as Lord indicate? (1 Corinthians 12:3)

    f. List the individual parts of the Gospel that one must believe in order to "believe on the Lord Jesus Christ." (1 Corinthians 15:1–4)

    g. Why is it not enough just to say, "I believe in Jesus" without believing in His death and resurrection?

    h. What is the one condition for salvation specified in Ephesians 2:8?

    i. How does this verse support Acts 16:31?

    j. Why is belief the only requirement for salvation? (Ephesians 2:9)

k. How does faith exclude boasting in anything but God's grace? (Romans 3:27–28)

2. Where was Paul when he wrote his letter to the Philippians? (Philippians 1:12–14)

   a. What theme do you find appearing throughout this letter?

   - 1:4

   - 1:18

   - 1:25

   - 2:2

   - 2:16

   - 2:17

   - 2:28

   - 3:1

   - 3:3

   - 4:1

   - 4:4

b. How was this theme to be seen in Paul and Silas's lives when imprisoned in Philippi? (Acts 16:25)

c. Compare the good things that happened when Paul was imprisoned in Philippi and later in Rome. (Acts 16:29–34; Philippians 1:14–18)

d. What lesson might you apply to your own life from his experiences?

DID YOU KNOW?

The Roman magistrates described in Acts 16 were attended by an official known as a lictor who carried a symbol of authority called a fasces. The fasces was a bundle of rods bound together into a handle from which protruded an axe blade. The axe blade was not used on accused people like Paul and Silas, but the rods were used to beat them. The modern expression "take a licking" comes from the Latin word lictor—the one who administered the beatings in Roman times. The fasces was bound with a red ribbon which was revived in modern times by the Italian leader Mussolini as the symbol for his "fascist" movement.

THE TALE OF TWO CITIES

Acts 17:1–15

In this lesson we follow Paul and his companions to two cities—one large and one small—with similar results.

OUTLINE

When we are attacked by opponents of Christianity, it is easy to get discouraged. Everywhere the apostle Paul went, he was attacked or opposed—and he took it as evidence of being in God's will. Wherever the Gospel is preached, some will embrace it and some will oppose it.

I. **The Response to the Gospel in Thessalonica**
   A. The City of Thessalonica
   B. The Congregation at Thessalonica
   C. The Converts at Thessalonica
   D. The Conflict at Thessalonica
   E. The Conclusion at Thessalonica

II. **The Response to the Gospel in Berea**
   A. Paul's Arrival in Berea
   B. Paul's Audience in Berea
   C. Paul's Accomplishment in Berea
   D. Paul's Adversaries in Berea

III. **The Response to the Gospel Today**
   A. The Communication of the Message
   B. The Reception of the Message
   C. The Content of the Message

I n the second half of the book of Acts, we find the apostle Paul causing riots or revivals wherever he went. And the most amazing thing about him is his endurance. He would preach in a city and suffer abuse at the hands of the populace (as he and Silas did in Philippi) and move right on to the next city and preach again.

In our culture it is hard for us to identify with the painful price paid by Paul and others in the first century and by many others in centuries since. But we may yet be tested in the same way in our own culture. We can learn from Paul and others that it is possible to be beaten in our bodies yet remain strong in our spirits. There will be plenty more opportunities to witness Paul's spiritual resolve as we follow him on his journeys.

THE RESPONSE TO THE GOSPEL IN THESSALONICA (17:1–10a)

In this lesson we follow Paul and his companions to two cities: first, Thessalonica, then Berea.

The City of Thessalonica (17:1)

There was no Jewish synagogue in Philippi, but there was in Thessalonica—and Paul made it his first stop upon arriving. As we have discussed in previous lessons, Paul's strategy in the cities to which he traveled was to go first to the synagogues to declare the gospel of Jesus. As he wrote in Romans 1:16, the gospel of Christ was "for the Jew first and also for the Greek."

I have learned that there are some 1,400 references to cities in the Bible, thirteen of which occupy a prominent place in the book of Acts. Two of them are Thessalonica and Berea. Paul passed through two small towns—Amphipolis and Apollonia—but did not stop. His strategy was always to preach in the largest cities and establish a church from which the Gospel could radiate to outlying locales.

Thessalonica was the main city in Macedonia, having a population of about 200,000. It had been founded in the Greek period by a brother-in-law of Alexander the Great. It was a port city and therefore a center of commerce, and still is today. (It is called Thessaloniki today.)

Paul went to the synagogue because there would be Jews as well as God-fearing Gentiles there. Gentiles recognized in the Jewish traditions a view of God not present in their pagan religions, and they gathered with the Jews at the synagogues to learn from the reading and teaching of the Old Testament Scriptures.

The Congregation at Thessalonica (17:2–3)

We find in Paul's ministry in Thessalonica an example of the strategies he used when delivering the Gospel.

1. The Strategy of Paul's Preaching (17:2–3a)

It's important to remember that Paul was trained to be a rabbi, and that gave him access to the "pulpit" in Jewish synagogues. He was learned and scholarly and so was allowed to speak, which he did for three Sabbaths in the Thessalonica synagogue. Paul didn't just preach—he reasoned, explained, and proved.

a. He Reasoned with Them

The Greek word for "reason" is *dialegomai* from which we get our English word "dialogue." Rather than being a monologue, Paul's style was to have a dialogue over the Scriptures when he visited a synagogue—questions and answers, give and take, back and forth, much as we might see in a seminar or class setting in our culture.

Paul was demonstrating what Peter wrote about in 1 Peter 3:15—being ready to give a defense to everyone who asks about the hope that you have, "with meekness and fear." Paul was comfortable in the dialogue mode because he was so knowledgeable and confident in what he believed.

b. He Explained to Them

The word "explain" means to open—the word that Luke used to describe how the eyes of the two men on the Emmaus road were "opened" when they realized they were with Jesus (Luke 24:31–32). Paul explained the Scriptures, or opened the Scriptures, so as to reveal their meaning to his listeners, much as (hopefully) preachers do today.

The whole point of teaching and preaching the Scriptures is to explain them—to make them clear to the listener. When communicators make their talks more about how scholarly they can sound instead of how clear they can make their subject, you know they aren't doing what Paul did. Paul's goal was for people—Jews and Gentiles alike—to see Jesus in the Old Testament, to see that He was the Jewish Messiah for whom Israel had been longing.

I heard a story about a young student who went to hear the great preacher George W. Truett at the First Baptist Church in Dallas, Texas. After the service the young man was heard to remark, "So that was the great George W. Truett, huh? He didn't use one word I didn't understand."

That young man unintentionally paid Pastor Truett the highest compliment possible: His sermons were clear and understandable. And I believe Paul's probably were, too.

c. He Proved to Them

Another way to say "proved" is that Paul "demonstrated" that "Christ had to suffer and rise again from the dead" (verse 3). This word means to give evidence. The only two kinds of evidence Paul could offer were the kinds he offered in passages like 1 Corinthians 15:5–7 and from the Old Testament. And to the audience in a Jewish synagogue, it was this latter evidence that was most important.

Paul could quote much of the Old Testament by heart (as is evidenced by his letters), and he no doubt wove the Old Testament prophecies into his message, demonstrating how Jesus of Nazareth was the fulfillment of each one. They had questions, and he answered them—dialoguing, explaining, giving evidence—in a convincing manner. And many of them came to believe.

2. The Substance of Paul's Preaching (17:3)

The substance of Paul's preaching was that Jesus is the Christ—"Christ" meaning Messiah. There was no need to convince the synagogue audience of the *fact* of the Messiah. They were looking for Him to come. What Paul taught over and over was that Jesus was the one they were looking for. Because the Jews wanted Messiah to come with a sword, Paul's biggest challenge was explaining why He came as a suffering, instead of a conquering, Servant. No doubt Paul spent much time in Isaiah 53, the key Old Testament passage on the fact that Messiah would come to suffer and bear the sins of His people.

The Converts at Thessalonica (17:4)

The result of Paul's weeks of teaching in the synagogue and in the city was significant: "Some of them were persuaded; and a great multitude of the devout Greeks, and not a few of the leading women, joined Paul and Silas." So there were Jews, Gentiles, and leading women of the city who became followers of Christ.

When Paul wrote back to the church at Thessalonica in his first letter to them, he reminded them of how they received the Word: "For this reason we also thank God without ceasing, because when you received the word of God which you heard from us, you welcomed it not as the word of men, but as it is in truth, the word of God, which also effectively works in you who believe" (1 Thessalonians 2:13). That verse says it all—from receiving to applying the Word. That's what should happen in our lives as well whether we hear the word from a preacher or discover it in our own personal Bible study.

The Conflict at Thessalonica (17:5)

Wherever the Gospel makes inroads into a society, there will be opposition—and there was in Thessalonica. The Jews in the city who didn't believe the Gospel "set the city in an uproar" and attacked the home where Paul and his companions had been staying. When they realized they couldn't defeat Paul by debating the Scriptures, they incited a mob ("evil men from the marketplace") to attack him and rid the city of his influence.

The Conclusion at Thessalonica (17:6–10a)

Jason, the brother at whose house Paul and his companions had been staying, bore the brunt of the mob's rage.

1. The Arrest of Jason (17:6a)

When the mob reached Jason's house, they did not find Paul, Timothy, and the others. They had been secreted out of the city by "the brethren" (verse 10). Not finding them, the crowd accused Jason and some of the others.

2. The Accusations Against Jason (17:6b–7)

The charge was that Jason was one of those who had "turned the world upside down" and acted "contrary to the decrees of Caesar, saying there is another king—Jesus." The world was already upside down! Paul and the others were trying to set it right. And Paul was certainly not promoting Jesus as a replacement for Caesar. As happened in Philippi, the charges were trumped up and false.

3. The Arraignment of Jason (17:8–10a)

The rulers of the city forced Jason to post a bond, probably to be forfeited if Paul and the others ever returned to Thessalonica. The officials knew that Paul was a Roman citizen, and they knew he had done nothing wrong. So they took action toward Jason, making him responsible to keep Paul and the others from ever disrupting the city again.

What the world thinks is disruptive (turning the world upside down) is actually God's work to set things right. The church's goal today should be to have the same effect on our world that Paul did on his.

THE RESPONSE TO THE GOSPEL IN BEREA (17:10b–15)

The brethren in Thessalonica smuggled Paul and his party out of town at night and sent them to Berea, a small town of only 6,000 people.

Paul's Arrival in Berea (17:10b)

Upon their arrival, Paul did what he always did: He went straight to the Jewish synagogue.

Paul's Audience in Berea (17:11)

Paul discovered in Berea a different culture than what he had encountered in Thessalonica.

1. The Dignity of the Bereans

The Bereans were more "fair-minded than those in Thessalonica," a phrase that probably mean several things. Overall, they likely had a more sophisticated, intellectual view of life. They were willing to hear Paul out and not condemn him immediately for his views and doctrine. In fact, Luke says the Bereans "received the word with all readiness."

2. The Discernment of the Bereans

But they didn't embrace what Paul said without verifying it for themselves: They "searched the Scriptures daily to find out whether these things were so" (verse 11b). Can you think of a higher compliment to pay anyone? No one should get a pass as a teacher or preacher! Everything I say or you say must be confirmed by studying the Word of God. Instead of rebelling or attacking, the Bereans simply studied the Word to see if what Paul said was true.

Paul's Accomplishment in Berea (17:12)

As a result of their study, "Many of them believed" (meaning the Jews), and a number of Greeks and prominent men and women as well. I find it encouraging to see how many of the elite members of various communities embraced the Gospel. With their intellect they studied and agreed that what Paul said was true. We should not be afraid to take the Gospel to the highest levels of our own society.

Paul's Adversaries in Berea (17:13–15)

As usual, not all agreed with the apostle. The Jews from Thessalonica had not been content to run Paul out of their town. They came to Berea as well to stir up that city against Paul. Some of the believers in Berea sent Paul out of the city immediately, leaving Timothy and Silas behind. The enemy of the Gospel, Satan, is never far from where it is being received—not in Paul's day or in ours. Paul was taken to Athens where Silas and Timothy soon joined him.

THE RESPONSE TO THE GOSPEL TODAY

The following are three lessons we can draw from Paul's experiences in Thessalonica and Berea.

The Communication of the Message

Paul was free, as we should be, to use more than one way to communicate the Gospel message. Paul reasoned, explained, demonstrated, preached, taught, persuaded—and those are just the words we find in Scripture.

The Reception of the Message

Here are the words we find used to describe what people did when Paul preached: They heard, accepted, anticipated, acknowledged, and applied it. And the Bereans also studied it to make sure they understood what it was saying. Even if we are already believers, we should do the same, using all our faculties to embrace the communicated Word of God.

The Content of the Message

Whether we are communicating or receiving the Word, the central focus should always and ultimately be Jesus Christ. That is the litmus test for a biblically-based message.

May the example of the apostle Paul and his companions stir you to deliver the message of God's grace to a needy world.

APPLICATION

After fleeing Thessalonica, Paul went to Athens, then to Corinth, where he penned 1 Thessalonians and sent it back to the believers he had just left a few weeks or months before. Answer the following questions based on 1 Thessalonians.

1. For what three things did Paul thank God regarding the Thessalonian believers? (1:3)

   - work of _____

   - labor of _____

   - patience of _____

   a. In what four ways did the Gospel come to the Thessalonians? (1:5)

      - in _____

      - in _____

      - in the _____ _____

      - in much _____

   b. To what "affliction" is Paul referring in verse 6? (Acts 17:5 ff.)

   c. What was the attitude of those who received the Gospel in spite of their suffering? (verse 6)

   d. How did Paul confirm the supernatural source of their joy? (verse 6; see Galatians 5:22)

e. What commendation did Paul make concerning the Thessalonians' faith in verses 7–8?

f. What three things were being said about the Thessalonians throughout Macedonia? (verses 9–10)

- They turned _____ .
- They served _____ .
- They were waiting _____ .

2. For at least how long were Paul and his companions in Thessalonica? (Acts 17:2)

a. Describe how they conducted themselves while they were in Thessalonica. (2:5–9)

b. What kind of parental role did Paul take toward the new believers? (2:7, 11)

c. What parallel circumstance did Paul cite to let them know that they were not alone in their suffering? (2:14–16)

3. Why didn't Paul return to Thessalonica after things had quieted down there? (2:17–18)

   a. Who did he send to them—and why? (3:2–3)

   b. What do you learn about suffering for the Gospel from Paul's words in 3:3b? (see Acts 14:22)

DID YOU KNOW?

A city ruler such as those in Thessalonica mentioned in Acts 17:6, 8 was called a *politarch* in Greek. That Greek word was suspect for centuries because it was found nowhere else in Greek literature. But in 1835, it was found in a Greek inscription on an arch in Thessalonica. The arch was destroyed in 1867, but the block of stone with the inscription was retrieved and is in the British Museum in London. The word was subsequently found in sixteen other inscriptions in towns in Macedonia and other places. The discovery was another verification of the historical reliability of the Bible. (*The NIV Study Bible, note on Acts 17:6.*)

on

THE SERMON ON THE UNKNOWN GOD

Acts 17:16–34

In this lesson we see Paul interacting with the intellectuals and philosophers of Athens.

OUTLINE

There are always those for whom the pursuit of truth is more important than the attainment of truth. And it was those people the apostle Paul encountered in Athens. They loved to spend their time debating the latest ideas. But Paul introduced them to truth incarnate: the resurrected Christ.

I. **The Situation Paul Discovered in Athens**
   A. The Idolatry of Athens
   B. The Intellectualism of Athens
   C. The Intolerance in Athens

II. **The Sermon Paul Delivered in Athens**
   A. The Reality of God
   B. The Recognition of God
      1. God Originated Everything
      2. God Is over Everything
      3. God Orders Everything
      4. God Ordains Everything

III. **The Summons Paul Issued in Athens**
   A. The Point That He Explains
   B. The Plea That He Extends

IV. **The Sequel to Paul's Visit to Athens**

S ometimes I think we take the apostle Paul for granted. Think about it: How many people in history have written a series of short letters that have been the source of countless books analyzing them and 2,000 years later, millions of people gathering together once a week to study what he wrote? Who could ever dream of leaving such a legacy?

It must be true that the apostle Paul is the greatest spiritual leader in history outside of Jesus Christ himself. Yet we who have been Christians for a number of years can take this great man for granted. We can fail to marvel at his obedience, his perseverance, his boldness, his spiritual and intellectual gifts from God, and his humble love for God's kingdom and King, the Lord Jesus Christ.

In this lesson we will look at one of the high-water marks in Paul's life—what has been called his "Sermon on Mars Hill" in the ancient city of Athens. It is a classic illustration of how to interact with those who do not know the true and living God, how to speak to them on their level and meet them where they are in their understanding of spiritual things.

We have witnessed Paul being thrown out of two cities, Berea and Thessalonica. He traveled from Berea to Athens, a 200-mile trip, passing many smaller towns along the way. Athens was a religious and philosophical crossroads in the ancient world, made famous by the Greek philosophers who taught there. So Paul went there to engage them on the subject of God's having revealed himself to mankind in the person of Jesus Christ.

THE SITUATION PAUL DISCOVERED IN ATHENS (17:16–21)

Paul arrived at Athens ahead of Silas and Timothy, but he wasted no time in getting started with his ministry: "Now while Paul waited for them at Athens, his spirit was provoked within him when he saw that the city was given over to idols" (verse 16).

Paul would have known about Athens just as we know about the famous, large cities in our day. He was familiar with the philosophers who had taught there—Aristotle, Socrates, Plato, Epicurus, Zeno, and others—and with the city's history of art, literature, philosophy, and politics. Corinth had replaced Athens as the leading commercial city in Greece, but Athens was still the leading cultural and intellectual center of the western world. If you wanted to engage in the world of ideas, Athens would be your destination.

It was also a religious city. There were around 10,000 people living in Athens when Paul was there, but it is said that there were some 30,000 statues of gods in the city—more gods than people! It was the proliferation of gods—idols—that provoked Paul the most. His heart was no doubt broken as he saw people bowing down before, and making offerings to, idols made of stone.

The Idolatry of Athens (17:16)

"Provoked" is from the Greek *paroxuno* which means to be provoked or upset within oneself. Paul was upset in his spirit because he witnessed the worship that God deserved being exercised toward idols of stone. The entire city was "given over to idols."

The Intellectualism of Athens (17:17–18)

Paul headed into the marketplace of Athens and to the Jewish synagogue to reason with whomever he could find. Paul was not afraid to give the reason for the hope that lay within him and was eager to ask others to defend their own beliefs (1 Peter 3:15). Paul was an initiator—he didn't wait for people to come to him. He waded into the marketplace of ideas in Athens armed with God's truth. He was probably in the synagogue on the Sabbath and in the markets the rest of the days.

The Epicureans, Stoics, and cynics were the three most popular schools of thought in Athens (verse 18). The goal of the Epicureans was to experience pleasure and avoid pain. They were materialists, with no thought of the spirit or eternal life. So, maximizing pleasure in this life was their highest aim.

The Stoics believed not in pleasure but in self-discipline, self-mastery. They believed self-mastery came by being indifferent to pleasure and pain. They were pantheists—everything is God and God is everything.

The Epicureans and Stoics in Athens referred to Paul as a "babbler" (*spermologos*, verse 18), a word that originally meant "seed picker" (note the word *sperm*, or seed, in *spermologos*). It evolved into a word that meant someone who picks at the seeds, or scraps, of ideas—collecting ideas and then passing them off as one's own intellectual property. They looked down on Paul, thinking he was not their intellectual equal.

The Intolerance in Athens (17:19–21)

As Paul talked to the intellectuals in Athens about Jesus and the Resurrection, they invited him to the Areopagus, or Mars Hill, so he could be interviewed by the leading intellects of the city. He was surrounded by the beautiful buildings of Athens, like the Parthenon, and by countless idols to the gods in the Greek pantheon. And before him stood the leading intellectual lights of the day. They wanted to know more of Paul's "new doctrine" (verse 19).

They weren't spiritually interested in Jesus, they were just intellectually interested in a belief system with which they were unfamiliar: "For all the Athenians and the foreigners who were there spent their time in nothing else but either to tell or to hear some new thing" (verse 21). Jesus was just another "god" to them, not the one true God. They were intolerant of anyone who said he had "the" truth.

THE SERMON PAUL DELIVERED IN ATHENS (17:22-26)

Paul was happy to meet their request and delivered a magnificent sermon while standing in the midst of Athens' philosophers and scholars.

The Reality of God (17:22-23)

Paul pointed out to them their religious interests (verse 22)—not hard to do in a town with 30,000 idols! And he mentioned one particular altar he had seen, inscribed to "THE UNKNOWN GOD" (verse 23).

That was his hook: "Therefore, the One whom you worship without knowing, Him I proclaim to you" (verse 23). He pointed out to them that, though they worshipped God, they did not know Him. He was proclaiming to them the God they did not know. There is no scientific proof that God exists, but there is evidence that He exists (Psalm 19:1-6; Romans 1:19-20). And Paul wanted the Athenians to know that the god they thought existed actually did exist and could be known by them.

Some intellectuals today say what the Athenians said: It is impossible to know God. If that's true, then the whole Bible is built on a false premise that it is possible to know Him (Deuteronomy 4:35; Psalm 9:10; Jeremiah 9:24; John 17:3). All who want to know God must begin with the belief that He exists and that He is knowable (Hebrews 11:6).

The Recognition of God (17:24-26)

Paul then describes God—who He is and what He has done—as evidence of the fact that He can be known. Paul cites four facts about God, facts that seem elementary to us. But remember, these Athenian scholars had no background in the Old Testament or Judaism, so Paul is starting with the basics.

1. God Originated Everything (17:24a)

The Epicureans believed that matter is eternal, that there was no Creator. And the Stoics believed that God was not personal but was the same as the creation (pantheism). But the Bible tells us that, "In the beginning God created the heavens and the earth" (Genesis 1:1) and that He did it through Jesus Christ (Ephesians 3:9; Colossians 1:16).

2. God Is over Everything (17:24b)

Not only is God the creator of everything, Paul said, He is "Lord of heaven and earth [and] does not dwell in temples made with hands" (verse 24)—an obvious reference to the man-made temples which surrounded them on the Areopagus.

Genesis 14:19 says that God is the "possessor of heaven and earth"; Psalm 24:1 says "the earth is the Lord's"; and Psalm 103:19 says God's "kingdom rules over all." The idea that one God, instead of thousands, ruled over all the earth would have been a new concept to the Athenians.

3. God Orders Everything (17:25)

God's rule results in everything being ordered according to His will: "He gives to all life, breath, and all things." God is the one who sustains life and meets every need of the creation (Romans 11:36; James 1:17). Paul is progressing logically: God creates, rules, and orders everything in all the world.

4. God Ordains Everything (17:26)

Paul's conclusion is also logical, that God ordains (appoints) everything: "And He has made from one blood every nation of men to dwell on all the face of the earth, and has determined their preappointed times and the boundaries of their dwellings."

This would have been highly offensive to the Greeks—the idea that the same "one blood" that flowed in them flowed also in the barbarians (non-Greeks). And the fact that God had put them where they are, instead of being a result of their own greatness, would likewise have been an offense. But Paul was not intimidated by Greek pride. He spoke the truth about God's primacy over all things.

THE SUMMONS PAUL ISSUED IN ATHENS (17:27–31)

Having presented the truth about God to the Athenian scholars, Paul went on to call them to respond to what he had said.

The Point That He Explains (17:27–29)

God's revelation of himself to humanity was "so that they should seek the Lord, in the hope that they might grope for Him and find Him" (verse 27).

To further connect with the Athenians, Paul quotes from two of their poets. First, when he says, "For we are also His offspring" (verse 28), he is quoting the Greek poet Aratus. He is pointing out that even one of their own poets had noted the fact that God is the creator of all. Paul is not saying that we are all God's children in a salvation sense (as in Romans 8:16–17).

Second, Paul's words, "For in Him we live and move and have our being" (verse 28) are based on the Greek poet Epimenides. God is the ruler of all, Paul is saying—we do not create Him; He has created us and ordained our place in this world.

Paul's subtle point was, standing in the midst of countless man-made idols, "Man does not create God. Your own poets have recognized that God has created man, not vice versa."

The Plea That He Extends (17:30–31)

Paul gets to the bottom line: "But now God commands all men everywhere to repent, because He has appointed a day on which He will judge the world in righteousness by the Man whom He has ordained. He has given assurance of this to all by raising Him from the dead."

"God has been patient with you," Paul was saying. "But now it is time for you to repent of worshipping false gods and worship the one, true God. The days of idol worship are over." Paul brings Christ into the picture by pointing out that the Resurrection is the proof that Christ is God's Man who will one day judge the world in righteousness.

This message of Paul's to the Athenians is a message worthy of repeating today. Our culture may not have created idols of wood and stone to worship, but we have certainly substituted other things in the place of worshipping God. Paul's warning of the judgment to come applies to us as well as to the Athenians to whom Paul first delivered it.

THE SEQUEL TO PAUL'S VISIT TO ATHENS (17:32–34)

As was normal, the reaction to Paul's sermon was mixed: A few people believed while others mocked. And some said they would like to hear Paul again "on this matter" (verse 32).

As far as we know, Paul never returned to Athens. But Paul's encounter with the intellectuals, scholars, and philosophers had a great impact on him and his future ministry. From Athens, Paul journeyed to Corinth, as we will see in our next lesson. And this was his mindset when he arrived in Corinth: "And I, brethren, when I came to you, did not come with excellence of speech or of wisdom declaring to you the testimony of God. For I determined not to know anything among you except Jesus Christ and Him crucified" (1 Corinthians 2:1–2).

Paul's experience in Athens had made him even more determined to stay focused on the centrality of the message of Christ. His time debating with the intellectuals in Athens did not result in a church being planted. But his Christ-centered time in Corinth did.

Even though Paul was a powerful intellect and a great debater, I believe his time in Athens reminded him that preaching "the foolishness" (1 Corinthians 1:21) of Christ crucified was his most powerful message. And it must remain the central focus of our message as well. Ultimately, mankind must decide about Jesus.

1. Read Isaiah 41:21–24. (Note: "Them" in verse 22 refers to the pagan nations and their idols.)

   a. What challenge did the Lord issue to "them" in verses 22–23?

   b. If the idols are truly gods, what should they be able to do? (verse 23)

   c. Since the idols do nothing, what is the conclusion? (verse 24)

   d. How does God describe those who choose to worship idols? (verse 24)

   e. What is an idol? (Isaiah 37:19)

   f. How are the people who worship idols like them? (Psalm 115:8; Isaiah 44:9)

2. What is the fundamental requirement for having a relationship with God? (Hebrews 11:6)

a. How has God made it possible for mankind to know about His existence? (Romans 1:19–20)

b. When did God begin revealing himself? (verse 20)

c. How do you think God's invisible attributes have been made visible? List a few examples. (verse 20)

d. In what condition has God's self-revelation left mankind?
Man is _____ .

e. Based on what you learned about the Athenians in this lesson, how do you think Romans 1:21–23 applies to them?

f. When mankind ignores God's self-revelation, to what three things does God give them over?
1. verse 24:

2. verse 26:

3. verse 28:

3. Read Psalm 19:1–6.

   a. What do the heavens declare about God? (verse 1)

   b. Give some examples of the kind of speech and knowledge the heaven's convey. (verse 2)

   c. How do verses 3–4, 6 support Romans 1:20?

   d. What part of creation speaks most clearly to you about God's existence and the kind of God He is?

4. In what was mankind created to glory? (Jeremiah 9:24)

DID YOU KNOW?

The Areopagus in Athens was two things: a rocky hill on the northwest side of the Acropolis, then the central and highest point in Athens. It was also the name of the council that met there, a sort of court responsible for dealing with matters of morality and the teachings espoused by those who, like Paul, lectured publicly to the crowds. It was *to* the Areopagus that Paul likely spoke when *on* the Areopagus. In Greek, Areopagus is *Areios pagos*. *Areios* in Greek mythology referred to Ares, the god of war, while *pagos* means "hill." So the Areopagus was the "Hill of Ares." The Romans referred to Ares as Mars; so in Roman times, the Areopagus became known as Mars Hill.

Dealing with Discouragement

Acts 18:1–17

In this lesson we witness God's provision that prevented Paul's discouragement.

OUTLINE

Discouragement is a human condition, but the Christian has resources no one else has: the provision and promises of God. When Paul faced a potentially discouraging situation in the city of Athens, God sustained him through people, proclamation, power, and due process.

I. **The Encouragement of Friends**

II. **The Evangelism of the Lost**

III. **The Empowerment of the Lord**
   A. He Had a Divine Assignment
   B. He Had Divine Assistance
   C. He Had a Divine Assurance
   D. He Had a Divine Appointment

IV. **The Experiences of His Enemies**

OVERVIEW

In the nearly four decades that I have been preaching the Gospel, there have been two occasions where I had to ask someone to fill the pulpit for me on Sunday morning for a particular reason. The reason wasn't illness or being out of town. The reason was discouragement—wrestling with personal and ministry issues that weighed on my spirit.

I don't mean depression—to the best of my knowledge, I have never been depressed. But I have been discouraged at times as I'm sure you have. I take some measure of comfort in knowing that my heroes in Scripture also experienced times of discouragement in their lives. They were great soldiers for the Lord, but they were also human—as you and I are.

Charles Haddon Spurgeon, a great preacher of another generation, once wrote: "Good men are promised tribulation in this world, and ministers may expect a larger share than others, that they may learn sympathy with the Lord's suffering people, and so may be fitting shepherds of an ailing flock." [1]

In this lesson we find Paul in Corinth, arriving there after many weeks of travel, ministry, and tribulation. His back was probably not yet completely healed from the beating he and Silas received in Philippi (Acts 16). And he had been confronted and persecuted almost everywhere he had been. And even when he was able to preach without being persecuted, as in Athens, only two people are named as having accepted the Gospel. (A few others believed but were unnamed.)

He would have had ample reason to wonder, while walking the fifty-three miles to Athens, "Why am I doing this?" Even the apostle Paul might have hit lonely stretches in his life when he wondered if all his effort was really making a difference. His words that he later wrote to the Corinthians suggest he was not happy with what had happened in Athens. He marshaled his best material and delivered it to the "thinkers" on Mars Hill with little result. And so he resolved to keep his focus on Christ alone in his preaching.

Corinth was not a place for a lonely, fatigued, beaten, on-the-edge-of-discouragement apostle to seek refreshment. In short, it was the most wicked city in Greece. In fact, to say that someone was a "Corinthian" meant he was an immoral person—base and wicked. It's easy to see why Paul said he came to Corinth "in weakness, in fear, and in much trembling" (1 Corinthians 2:3).

Fortunately, Paul was not alone. God was with him and knew exactly how he felt and provided friends in Corinth who could be a source of encouragement to Paul. God always knows our needs and is traveling ahead of us to arrange support and refreshment.

THE ENCOURAGEMENT OF FRIENDS (18:1–5a)

When Paul arrived in Corinth alone, he met a Jew named Aquila, and Aquila's wife, Priscilla. This couple had recently come to Corinth "from Italy" because the emperor Claudius had banished Jews from Rome. They had probably been converted to Christ in Rome by Jews who returned from Pentecost in Jerusalem. Aquila and Priscilla were tentmakers—the same trade as Paul.

So Paul entered the city knowing no one, and God put in his path a couple of believers who shared his occupation and with whom he could live. Paul did not take money from Christians for his ministry but worked at tentmaking to support himself (1 Corinthians 4:12a; 2 Corinthians 11:7; 1 Thessalonians 2:9). This was not a coincidence. It was the providential hand of God, providing for the needs of the apostle (Philippians 4:19). This relationship served Paul well in Corinth and into the future: In three different cities, over a period of sixteen years, Paul and Aquila and Priscilla ministered together.

Paul taught every Sabbath in the synagogue in Corinth "and persuaded both Jews and Greeks" (verse 4). And then Silas and Timothy arrived in Corinth from Macedonia, bringing a gift for Paul from the churches (2 Corinthians 11:9). It was likely that offering which allowed Paul to minister full time in Corinth and not rely on his tentmaking for support. I meet faithful bivocational pastors all over the country who work at regular jobs during the week and then preach in small churches on the weekend. The churches aren't large enough to support them full time, so they have a "tentmaking" ministry like Paul. I know the Lord will reward these faithful ministers for what they do in spite of not being able to be supported full-time.

So Paul's situation changed dramatically from when he first arrived in Corinth. He met Aquila and Priscilla, lived with them, worked with them, was reunited with his coworkers Timothy and Silas, and received a monetary gift of support—a love offering—from those to whom he had ministered in Macedonia. God is a God of encouragement—in Paul's life and in ours—if we will wait patiently for Him to meet our needs.

THE EVANGELISM
OF THE LOST (18:5b-8)

God also encouraged Paul in another way: allowing the apostle to see souls converted to Christ. I have found in my own life that there is nothing more encouraging to a discouraged minister of the Gospel than to share the good news with someone and see them respond in faith.

As Paul preached in the synagogue, he saw division: Some believed and some didn't. But when Silas and Timothy arrived, Paul took a harder line. When the Jews began to blaspheme the name of Christ, Paul shook out his garments (what the Jews would do to a Gentile as an act of rejection) and told them their blood was upon their own heads—he was leaving to take the Gospel to the Gentiles (verse 6).

Paul didn't leave the Jews for good, of course. It was a way to say to them that God's patience had its limits. If they weren't interested in embracing their Messiah, he would go to the Gentiles and offer Him to them. As a result, a number of Corinthians were saved, including Justus, a Gentile who lived next to the synagogue, and Crispus, the ruler of the synagogue. They, along with others, believed and were baptized (verse 8). This would have been a great encouragement to Paul.

THE EMPOWERMENT
OF THE LORD (18:9-11)

The apostle Paul had a vision from the Lord six times in his life, all recorded in the book of Acts. They were always in response to a need Paul had, and this time was no different. Paul needed encouragement and confirmation, and God brought it to him in a vision.

He Had a Divine Assignment (18:9)

In the vision Paul received an assignment: "Do not be afraid, but speak, and do not keep silent." It seemed every time Paul opened his mouth and spoke, he got in trouble: jail, beatings, persecution, and the like. He needed to have his mission and ministry confirmed, and that is what this vision supplied.

He Had Divine Assistance (18:10)

In spite of his human companions, Paul needed to know that there was divine assistance available. That's why God said, "For I am with you."

This was the same message Joshua received from the Lord when he was about to lead Israel into Canaan to inherit the land: "As I was with Moses, so I will be with you. I will not leave you nor forsake you" (Joshua 1:5). Paul's consolation in every difficult situation he faced was knowing that God was with him. Even near the end of his life, he cited God as being the person and presence that had never deserted him (2 Timothy 4:17).

One of the names of Jesus, given before He was born, was Immanuel, "which is translated, 'God with us'" (Matthew 1:23). And by the presence of the Holy Spirit in the life of every believer, we are assured of God's presence with us. There is never a time when we are alone if we are a child of God.

He Had a Divine Assurance (18:10b)

Paul then received something that must have been a great relief to him, given his experience in previous cities: "And no one will attack you to hurt you."

I can't get out of my mind the fact that Paul's back was probably still healing from the severe beating he and Silas received in Philippi. He probably lived with the dreadful thought of being beaten again on a not-yet-healed part of his body. But God relieved him of that concern with a promise that he would not be attacked or hurt in Corinth.

He Had a Divine Appointment (18:10c)

Finally, the last promise given to Paul might have seemed a little odd to the apostle: "For I have many people in this city."

When Paul arrived in Corinth, there probably were very few, if any, Christians in the city besides Aquila and Priscilla. And they had only recently resettled there from Rome. But God told Paul that there were many of His people in the city—before they had ever made decisions for Christ.

This promise raises the theological doctrine of election— the biblical truth that God sovereignly chooses, according to His purpose and plan, those who will respond to the preaching of the Gospel. God knew there were some in Corinth who would receive Christ by faith, foreordained by Him to believe.

Again, the words of Charles Spurgeon are helpful:

This should be a great encouragement since God has among the vilest an elect people who must be saved. When you take the Word to them, you do so because God has ordained you to be the messenger of life to their souls, and they must receive it. . . . They are Christ's property. . . . God is not unfaithful to forget the price His Son paid. . . . Tens of thousands of redeemed ones are not regenerated yet, but regenerated they must be; and this is our comfort, when we go forth to them with the quickening Word of God.[2]

Paul's job was to be the messenger of the Gospel to those who would be saved—and it is our job as well. God has people where you live who have been chosen to believe, but they must have a preacher to deliver the Word to them (Romans 10:14). And you, and other believers in your town, must be the preacher.

When we read stories in Scripture like this one about Paul's vision, we think there is nothing there for us. We're not apostles, and God doesn't send us visions in the night to encourage us. But let me remind you: It is not visions we are after—it is encouragement by the Word of the Lord. And God sends us His Word in many, many ways. Just because it does not come in a vision does not make it less true and less applicable. Many times I have heard this story from people I meet as I travel across the country: They were struggling through a discouraging situation when they "happened" to hear me preaching on the radio, and the Word of the Lord at that moment was just what they needed! That happens innumerable times around the world every day—but not just through my preaching. Wherever God's faithful ministers are proclaiming His Word, the Spirit causes it to fall on the ears and into the heart of a person who needs just such an encouraging word at that moment.

So live with your spiritual eyes and ears open—especially your eyes as you seek out God's Word in your own personal Bible study each day. God is ready to encourage you with a word of hope, but you have to be in a place to receive it.

THE EXPERIENCES OF HIS ENEMIES (18:12–17)

God kept His promises to Paul by thwarting the plans of Paul's enemies. Those Jews who tried to discourage Paul by bringing him before the proconsul (ruler) had their case thrown out of court. Gallio told the Jews, "This is a religious matter, not a matter of Roman law. Go solve this problem yourselves" (paraphrase, verse 15). In fact, Gallio said there was no "wrongdoing" or "wicked crimes" that had been committed. Paul was completely vindicated and suffered no harm, just as God had promised.

I wasn't there, obviously, but just reading about how God provided for Paul is a great encouragement to me! This story reminds me afresh that God knows our needs, that we are His children, that He has prearranged resources and people to provide for our needs; that He will give us renewed courage when we are tempted toward discouragement. And most of all, I am reminded of the value and necessity of receiving the promises of God as a shield against the situations in which we are tempted to despair.

If you are in a place of discouragement right now, ask God to send you a fresh promise through His Word. And then prepare for God to fulfill all of His promises to you.

Notes:

1. Charles Haddon Spurgeon, "The Minister's Fainting Fits," *Lectures to My Students, First Series* (Grand Rapids: Baker, n.d.), 168.

2. W. H. Griffith Thomas, *Outline Studies in the Acts of the Apostles* (Grand Rapids: Wm. B. Eerdmans Publishing Co., 1960), 366.

1. Read 2 Corinthians 1:3–11. (Note: The suffering Paul refers to in these verses did not occur in Corinth, but gives insight into Paul's defense against discouragement and despair.)

    a. How did Paul refer to God? "The Father of _____
    and God of all _____." (verse 3)

    b. What is a by-product of the comfort God extends to those in pain? (verse 4)

    c. If we are to _____ others, we must ourselves be
    _____ by God. If we are to be _____
    by God, the implication is that we are experiencing
    _____ of some sort. (verse 4)

    d. If we experience suffering for Christ, what will we also experience? (verse 5)

    e. Describe the extent of Paul's trouble while in Asia. (verse 8)

    f. What did Paul learn through his near-death experience? (verse 9b)

g. Why does God allow us to experience discouragement and trouble at times? (verse 10)

h. What human means does God use to bring about the comfort and deliverance of those who are in pain? (verse 11)

2. Read 2 Corinthians 4:7–12.

a. What does "earthen vessels" suggest about our human strength? (How easily can a clay pot be broken?) (verse 7)

b. In spite of our fragile human state, with God we are . . . (verses 8–9)

- _____–_____ on every side, yet not _____ .

- _____ , but not in _____ .

- _____ , but not _____ .

- _____ down, but not _____ .

c. Why does God allow us to experience the "dying" of Jesus in our human experience? (verses 10–11)

d. How might the life of Jesus be manifested in you when you are tempted to be discouraged?

3. What promise did Jesus make to His disciples when He sent them out into the world? (Matthew 28:20)

   a. How is Christ's presence actually realized in us? (John 14:16–17)

   b. Why is Christ in you a source of hope in times of discouragement? (Joshua 1:5; Colossians 1:27)

DID YOU KNOW?

In the Roman period, Athens was the intellectual center of Greece, but Corinth was the most important city. Corinth was a seaport and thus a crossroads for commerce, paganism, and vice. It was also the site of the Isthmian Games. Corinth had something no other Greek city had: the temple of Aphrodite, the goddess of love. The temple was situated above the city on the Acropolis, or Acrocorinthus, and housed a reported one thousand prostitutes known as "sacred servants." Plying their immoral trade was how they worshipped the goddess—a practice known throughout the pagan cultures of the ancient world.

LESSONS IN LEADERSHIP

Acts 18:18–19:10

In this lesson we draw three principles of ministry from the expansion of the church in Acts.

OUTLINE

The narrative portions of Scripture provide deep historical records of the times and events they cover. But they are not just a record of history—they are a record of God's interaction with man over time. As such they provide insight and instruction for those who read with an eye to learn.

I. **The Principle of Cultural Accommodation**

II. **The Principle of Spiritual Motivation**
   A. Paul: Discipling the Believers
   B. Apollos: Defending the Faith
      1. He Was a Polished Speaker
      2. He Was Powerful in the Scriptures
      3. He Was Passionate in Spirit
      4. He Was Precise in His Sermons
   C. Aquila and Priscilla: Deepening the Understanding

III. **The Principle of Progressive Revelation**

D o you remember from a previous lesson how Paul was "forbidden by the Holy Spirit to preach the word in Asia" (Acts 16:6)? In this lesson we are going to see Paul returning to the region from which he was originally barred. It is a good lesson to us today that sometimes God's "No's" are not permanent—sometimes they are "Not now's." If we will submit to God's timetable, we will often see our original desire come to pass, but at a better time.

When Paul left Corinth (Acts 18:18), he took with him his new friends in the faith, Aquila and Priscilla. He had likely regained his strength and healed his wounds in Corinth; but as a missionary evangelist with a calling to fulfill, he could not stay put in one place for long. So he left Corinth and sailed for home—Syrian Antioch and the church that had originally sent him and Barnabas out as missionaries.

He stopped in Ephesus on the way, but would soon return and stay there for two years. There are three principles of ministry that emerge from this period in Paul's life that we can apply to our own ministries today.

THE PRINCIPLE OF CULTURAL ACCOMMODATION (18:18b–21b)

At the port city of Cenchrea (just east of Corinth), Paul had his hair cut before setting sail, "for he had taken a vow" (verse 18b).

Paul had lived his whole life as a Jew, and there were practices that were embedded deep in his heart. One of them was the Nazirite vow, something into which truly committed Jews like Paul would enter (Galatians 1:13–14). When he became a Christian, Paul stopped depending on his Jewish practices to earn him favor before God; but that did not mean he dropped all the cultural aspects of his former faith. Paul was still a Jew—but a Jew who had accepted the Jewish Messiah. Even today we speak of "Jewish Christians" or "Messianic Christians." After thousands of years, the heritage of Judaism is still distinctive in the world.

The Nazirite vow was established in the Old Testament in Numbers 6:1–23. It was an act of consecration to God for one's whole life (for example, Samson) or for a temporary period of time (as in Paul's case). Perhaps Paul's vow had been as an act of gratitude to God for safety and fruitfulness in ministry—we aren't told the specific reason. But part of the vow involved not cutting one's hair; so when Paul had his hair cut in Cenchrea, it was a sign that the time of his vow was over.

Nazirites couldn't drink alcohol, cut their hair, or be defiled by a dead body. When the vow was complete, the Nazirite was to come to the door of the tabernacle (later, the temple), cut his hair, and place it on the sacrificial fire that burned there (Numbers 6:13, 18).

Why did Paul, no longer constrained by the ceremonial law of Judaism, enter into this vow as a Christian? Some believe Paul was in error, even sin, by entering into this vow. But I believe not. Remember his strategy: The Gospel was to the Jew first, then to the Greek (Romans 1:16). In every city, his first destination was the Jewish synagogue or wherever Jews worshipped if there was no synagogue. I believe as Paul envisioned going to Ephesus that he saw the vow as another bridge to his Jewish kinsmen, another contact point for spreading the Gospel to them. He was willing to become all things to all men in order to save some (1 Corinthians 9:19–23).

Christians today should learn a lesson from the apostle Paul. There are plenty of areas in which we can identify with non-Christian friends without violating our own conscience or our righteous standing before God. I recall one time sitting for several hours in a cloud of smoke to share the Gospel with a non-Christian couple we invited into our home. We didn't even have ashtrays, so we used saucers from the kitchen. It was not a pleasant evening physically, but we had decided we could put up with some smoke for the opportunity to tell that couple about Jesus.

That's the principle of accommodation: accommodating ourselves to others' needs for the sake of the Gospel without compromising our own personal practices. Many Christians today are so rigid in their beliefs that they miss the opportunities to build bridges into the non-Christian world.

THE PRINCIPLE OF SPIRITUAL MOTIVATION (18:21c–28)

In this passage we find three beautiful illustrations of spiritual leadership being worked out in the main characters: Paul, Apollos, and Aquila and Priscilla.

Paul: Discipling the Believers (18:21c–23)

In three short verses we find Paul covering hundreds and hundreds of miles: from Ephesus to Caesarea to Jerusalem to Syrian

Antioch and then back into Asia Minor. His goal in returning to Asia Minor? "Strengthening the disciples" (verse 23) in the churches he had planted earlier.

Returning to Jerusalem and the church in Antioch marked the end of Paul's second missionary journey. Leaving Antioch and going into Asia Minor was the beginning of his third major journey. This was to be a long trip, taking Paul through Asia Minor and back into Europe, visiting all the churches he had planted to strengthen them in the faith. Paul was committed to two things: seeing people come to faith and then building them in the faith.

Apollos: Defending the Faith (18:24–26a)

This is our first encounter with a believer named Apollos, a Jew who was born in Alexandria, Egypt. Paul met Apollos after making his way through Asia Minor and arriving in Ephesus.

1. He Was a Polished Speaker

Luke tells us that Apollos was "an eloquent man and mighty in the Scriptures" (verse 24), "mighty" being the Greek adjective *dunamai*, the same word used to describe the power of the Holy Spirit and from which our word dynamite comes.

2. He Was Powerful in the Scriptures

Skipping ahead to verse 28, we find that Apollos "vigorously refuted the Jews publicly, showing from the Scriptures that Jesus is the Christ." The word "vigorously" is rare in the New Testament (see Luke 23:10), and comes from the word that means "to stretch." Apollos stretched the Jews to their intellectual limits as he crushed their arguments.

John Broadus wrote a famous book on preaching. Nine days before he died, he said to his students, "Gentlemen, if this were the last time I should ever be permitted to address you, I would feel amply repaid for consuming the whole hour endeavoring to impress upon you these two things: true piety and, like Apollos, to be men 'mighty in the Scriptures.'" No Christian could have a greater legacy than that.

Many young pastors and preachers today are more enamored with growing mega-churches by the use of clever marketing and management principles than they are with being mighty in the Scriptures. But cultural relevancy never saved anyone. As Paul has demonstrated, we have to be in touch with our cultural surroundings;

but as both he and Apollos proved, being mighty in the Scriptures is what changes lives.

3. He Was Passionate in Spirit

Apollos was also "fervent in spirit" (verse 25), meaning he was "boiling hot" (Greek *zeo*, to boil). This is an amazing combination of qualities to find in one person. It is no wonder that he made an impact in the early church (1 Corinthians 1:12; 3:4–5, 22; 4:6; Titus 3:13).

4. He Was Precise in His Sermons

Apollos "spoke and taught accurately the things of the Lord" (verse 25)—so far as he knew. Apollos' knowledge of the Gospel was apparently limited to the fact that John the Baptist had been proclaiming the coming of "the Lamb of God who takes away the sin of the world!" (John 1:29). It appears that he might not have even been a Christian at this point, though all he needed was someone to tell him how.

Apollos illustrates a principle in the Word of God: Those who have a hunger to know God will be given what they lack in knowledge (John 7:17). Apollos followed the light that he had, and then God sent him more light in the persons of Aquila and Priscilla.

Aquila and Priscilla: Deepening the Understanding (18:26b–28)

Paul was a discipler, and Apollos was a defender—and Aquila and Priscilla were those who deepened the understanding of others. They were the ones who pulled Apollos aside and filled him in on everything that had happened since John the Baptist had been preaching repentance and announcing the coming of the Messiah. They "explained to him the way of God more accurately" (verse 26).

Apollos was apparently a humble man, receiving the gentle correction and understanding that Aquila and Priscilla offered. When he wanted to leave Ephesus and sail across to Achaia (he ended up in Corinth—Acts 19:1), he received a letter of commendation and introduction to the church there and continued his influential ministry, though now more accurately.

Aquila and Priscilla were such a godly couple and wise counselors. We need people like them in the church today who will gently put their arms around younger or less mature believers and guide them in a scriptural path.

THE PRINCIPLE OF PROGRESSIVE
REVELATION (19:1-7)

The third principle for ministry that we find here concerns progressive revelation. It occurs in a context that has caused much trouble to some believers because of what happened when Paul arrived in Ephesus.

Paul discovered a pocket of "disciples" (verse 1) who had received the baptism of John the Baptist (like Apollos) but had never heard of the Holy Spirit. There were people throughout the Mediterranean world who were at various stages of knowledge and understanding in spiritual matters. The Holy Spirit had come at Pentecost but not everyone had heard that. (Think about how slowly news traveled in that day compared to today!)

So Paul explained the Gospel of Christ to them and baptized them in His name according to the formula of the Great Commission (Matthew 28:19). (Note again how promptly baptism occurred following belief in Christ.) When this group of 12 men were baptized that day, "The Holy Spirit came upon them, and they spoke with tongues and prophesied" (verse 6). And thus the point of conflict.

Some Bible teachers today use this passage as a template for saying that all post-Pentecost Christians should speak in tongues and prophesy when they are saved and are baptized by the Holy Spirit into the body of Christ.

I can do no better than one of my former seminary professors, Dr. Charles Ryrie, has done to explain what happened:

When Paul arrived in Ephesus on the third missionary journey, he discovered a group of twelve disciples of John the Baptist. He asked them if they had received the Holy Spirit when they believed John's message. When they confessed complete ignorance of the Spirit, Paul explained to them the preparatory ministry of John in relation to Christ. When they heard and understood the difference, they believed and were baptized in the name of Christ, at which time they did receive the Spirit. Whatever problem might seem to be raised by the fact that these men did not receive the Spirit under the preaching of John is solved by remembering that they did not become believers in Jesus by believing John's message, for they obviously did not even understand the meaning of John's message and baptism (verses 3–4), to say nothing of the Christian message. But when they did understand and believe in Jesus, then they received the Spirit immediately.[1]

Believers in Christ receive the Holy Spirit only once and at one specific time: when they believe. That is what happened to these men in Ephesus. As the Gospel spread from Jerusalem after Pentecost, the same manifestations occurred as occurred there—tongues and miraculous gifts—for purposes of validating the consistency of the revelation from God. It happened in Jerusalem through Peter, again with the Gentiles through Peter (Acts 10), in Samaria through Philip, and in Ephesus through Paul. As the transitional period of the spread of the Gospel and the gift of the Spirit concluded, and the church became united across a broad geographical and ethnic spectrum, the miraculous, authenticating gifts ceased.

When the disciples of John in Ephesus (again, like Apollos) heard the complete Gospel of Christ and believed and were baptized, they received the Holy Spirit with the manifestations appropriate to the progress of God's revelation in that day. It's interesting that as Paul began to write his letters to the churches, he never spoke of the miraculous gifts as being necessary. But he did cite the fruit of the Spirit (Galatians 5:22–23) as being evidence of the presence of the Spirit.

These three principles of leadership in ministry will guide us: cultural accommodation, spiritual motivation, and progressive revelation. As we watch the church expand in these chapters of Acts, we should read it not just as history but as a pattern of ministry to follow. What worked for the church in the first century will work as well in the twenty-first.

Note:

1. Charles Ryrie, *The Holy Spirit* (Chicago: Moody Press, 1963), 72.

APPLICATION

1. Read 1 Corinthians 9:19–23.

    a. What seeming contradiction in his life does Paul note in verse 19a?

    b. Why did Paul make himself "a servant to all?" (verse 19b)

    c. How is the Nazirite vow Paul took an illustration of what he says in verse 20?

    d. How is Acts 17:16–31 an illustration of verse 21?

    e. How is Romans 14:1–15:1 an example of Paul's taking "the weak" into consideration? (verse 22a)

    f. Why is verse 22b not a statement of compromise or weakness on Paul's part?

    g. How would it be easy to abuse this principle when it comes to lifestyle decisions?

h. Cite an example of how you have become a servant (verse 19) to non-Christians or "weak" (Romans 14) Christians for the sake of the Gospel?

i. Was there a Christian who served you in some way that helped open your eyes to the Gospel?

2. Where did Apollos go after being instructed by Aquila and Priscilla at Ephesus? (Acts 18:27–19:1)

a. What stature does it appear Apollos had gained in Corinth? (1 Corinthians 1:12)

b. To what would you attribute Apollos' leadership? (Acts 18:24, 27–28)

c. Look at 1 Corinthians 16:12. How badly does it appear the Corinthian believers missed him?

d. How does "helping" (serving) others almost always result in a bond of endearment being established? (Acts 18:27)

e. What spiritual gift(s) would you say Apollos had?
   (Cf. 1 Corinthians 12:8–10, 28)

f. What spiritual gift(s) has God given you? How would
   you compare the use of your gift(s) with the way Apollos
   used his?

DID YOU KNOW?

Apollos was from Alexandria, a city on the Mediterranean coast of Egypt that was founded by Alexander the Great in 322 B.C. It served as the capital of Egypt until Egypt was conquered by Arabs in A.D. 641. It was an important cultural center due to its university (modeled on Athens') and its library. The library was the greatest in the ancient world, containing between a half-million and one million books and scrolls. It was supposedly destroyed by fire more than once, causing the loss of untold ancient manuscripts. The lighthouse of Alexandria was one of the Seven Wonders of the Ancient World, and the Greek translation of the Old Testament, the Septuagint, was completed there between the third and first centuries B.C.

THE PROOF OF THE GOSPEL

Acts 19:11–41

*In this lesson we see what happens
when God's work makes progress in the world.*

OUTLINE

When churches are enjoying peace and comfort, they often take it
as a sign of God's blessing. But we discover from the book of Acts
that when God's work is being done effectively, things are not
always so comfortable. Power and progress always bring pretense
and persecution.

  I.   **If It Is God's Work, There Will Be Proof**

 II.   **If It Is God's Work, There Will Be Pretense**

III.   **If It Is God's Work, There Will Be Power**

IV.   **If It Is God's Work, There Will Be Progress**

 V.   **If It Is God's Work, There Will Be Persecution**
        A. The Reason for the Persecution
        B. The Reality of the Persecution
        C. The Relief of the Persecution

W hen the Gospel moves into the world, things happen! They happened in the first century in Ephesus, and they happen in the towns and cities where we live today. As we conclude our study of Acts 19 and Paul's two-year stay in Ephesus, we'll find five things happening that take place whenever God's work is being accomplished. If you are in a place where the Gospel is advancing, I believe you will recognize some or all of them.

IF IT IS GOD'S WORK, THERE WILL BE PROOF (19:11–12)

Amazing things happened through Paul's ministry in Ephesus. People were healed of illnesses and demonization by being touched by "handkerchiefs or aprons" that had touched Paul's body. These miracles, just as with the miracles of Jesus, were authenticating signs of the veracity of the Word that was being preached.

God's Word clearly points out how miracles were given by God through His servants— His Son and His apostles: Acts 2:22; 2 Corinthians 12:12; Hebrews 2:3–4. When people ask me why we don't see miracles today as were seen in the first century, the answer is clear: Today we have the Word of God. God's messengers today are not authenticated by signs and wonders. They are authenticated by whether or not their message is consistent with the Word.

Even Luke was amazed at the miracles in Ephesus—he called them "unusual miracles" (verse 11). The miracles of healing through pieces of Paul's clothing were never intended to set a pattern for ministry today. They were, by definition, "unusual miracles." Yet today some unscrupulous ministers will offer to send out a cloth of some kind that has been prayed over, supposedly able to work miracles, in exchange for a financial gift. We don't know why God chose to work such an unusual miracle in Ephesus through Paul, but he did. Perhaps it was because of the pagan brands of magic so common in the city that there was a necessity to overpower them with the true power of God. A similar thing happened to Jesus on occasion— people being healed as a result of touching His garment (Matthew 9:20; Mark 6:56).

God certainly used an unusual way to speak to the people of Ephesus. But how do we transfer this to today? What would be the equivalent of something so dramatic? I believe when the people of God demonstrate faith and service in ways the world doesn't understand that it has the same dramatic effect on the spread of the Gospel.

Our church has been in its current location for twenty-one years. It has taken the surrounding community a while to get used to our growing presence and the traffic jams on Sunday. But in recent years, they have come to understand us a bit better. When wildfires swept through our community and our church members fanned out taking food and supplies and comfort to those who were affected, people noticed. We didn't do it so they would notice, but their understanding of us deepened as a result along with their appreciation for our faith.

God has called the church to reach out and touch the world just as Jesus and the apostles touched their world with signs and wonders. Our signs and wonders today are love and compassion and a servant's heart as we display Christ to the world. Practicing the Great Commission (take the Gospel into all the world) and the Great Commandment (love your neighbor) is God's two-pronged approach to impacting our world.

IF IT IS GOD'S WORK, THERE WILL BE PRETENSE (19:13-16)

Everywhere God's truth is making an impact, there will be pretenders and counterfeiters who try to take advantage of peoples' openness. That's what happened in Ephesus when a group of Jewish exorcists tried to use the name of Jesus to take authority over evil spirits.

Magicians of that day would grab at any advantage. When they saw the power of Paul—even of his clothes—to work miracles, they tried to use Jesus' name as a magical incantation—like saying "Abracadabra" as modern magicians do when performing a trick. But when they spoke the name of Jesus to the spirits, a demon spoke back: "Jesus I know, and Paul I know; but who are you?" (verse 15) How comical! The evil spirits knew that Paul and Jesus had true authority but that the Jewish exorcists were imposters. In fact, the demonized man attacked the exorcists and "overpowered them, and prevailed against them, so that they fled out of that house naked and wounded" (verse 16). Amazing!

James 2:19 says that "the demons believe—and tremble!" They are well aware of the source of true spiritual authority in the spiritual realm and on earth. And to Jesus, and His representatives, they have to submit. But they owed no submission to people who were using Jesus' name but did not really know Him nor had been commissioned by Him.

There is a warning here for all who would pretend to have spiritual authority or a spiritual presence, who do not know the true spiritual authority, Jesus Christ.

IF IT IS GOD'S WORK, THERE WILL BE POWER (19:17–19)

As a result of this power encounter in Ephesus, the power of the Gospel spread throughout the city. Many were converted to Christ and they came confessing their involvement in magic and the black arts. They burned all their magic books and paraphernalia, items that had a value of 50,000 pieces of silver (verse 19). James Montgomery Boice wrote this about that number: "Luke puts the value of the objects at fifty thousand drachmas. A drachma was a day's wage. So if we can assume that a day's wage in the United States in our time is roughly a hundred dollars (annual income $25,000), the equivalent of fifty thousand drachmas would be about five million dollars in our currency. That may be a high estimate, but by any estimate, it was a large sum of money."[1]

Would the power of God have even greater effect today if Christians who are involved with activities they shouldn't be brought all their paraphernalia together and burned it in an act of repentance? It's something to consider.

When the Gospel is unleashed with genuine spiritual reality, there will be power—and the power will be seen in genuine repentance and changed lives.

IF IT IS GOD'S WORK, THERE WILL BE PROGRESS (19:20–22)

"So the word of the Lord grew mightily and prevailed" (verse 20). When God is at work, there will be progress; and the Gospel definitely made progress in Ephesus.

What we count as progress in the modern church cannot compare to the rapid progress made in the first century. But we could see that kind of progress if the Word of God were allowed to prevail over sin and carnality—especially in the church. If the world ever sees the church get serious about itself, they will get serious about the church. And the faithful preaching of, and submission to, the Word of God is the key. It is living and active (Hebrews 4:12) and is used by the Spirit to bring about conviction and confession. And progress is the result.

IF IT IS GOD'S WORK, THERE WILL BE PERSECUTION (19:23–41)

Now we come to what we have already seen several times in Acts: When God is at work, there will be opposition and persecution.

The Reason for the Persecution (19:23–27)

A great riot broke out against Paul and his coworkers, at the root of which was money. A silversmith in Ephesus named Demetrius who made small images of the goddess Diana was upset because of the revenue he and his fellow craftsmen were losing due to the spiritual revival in Ephesus. Worshippers of Diana would purchase the small votives and leave them at the temple of Diana as an offering to the goddess. As long as people were worshipping Diana, the silversmiths made money. When they stopped, the silversmiths lost money. Their concern was not religion, it was economics. People were being saved and ceasing their worship of man-made gods and goddesses.

In order to generate anger toward the Christian workers among the general populace, Demetrius claimed that the Gospel was going to undermine the religious heritage of Ephesus and the entire region. He stirred up the crowds by suggesting that the temple of Diana would eventually fall into ruins. This temple was one of the seven wonders of the ancient world—425 feet by 220 feet in size, surrounded by 127 white marble columns, each 62 feet high. This temple that took 220 years to build was in danger of becoming a relic, said Demetrius, unless they did something to stop the progress of "the Way" (verse 23).

While the silversmiths were mostly concerned about their livelihood, they stirred up the whole city by appealing to their sense of tradition—the place of Diana's temple in the city.

The Reality of the Persecution (19:28–34)

Demetrius was successful—the crowds in the city "were full of wrath and cried out, saying, "Great is Diana of the Ephesians!" (verse 28)—for two solid hours (verse 34)!

The Christian brothers in the city would not let Paul get anywhere near the commotion for fear of harm coming to him. A Jew named Alexander tried to address the crowd, but he was shouted down and not allowed to speak. Two believers, Gaius and

Aristarchus, were grabbed and taken into the open-air theatre where the crowd had gathered, but Paul was hidden by the believers.

Paul was right when he later wrote to the Corinthians, "For a great and effective door has opened to me, and there are many adversaries" (1 Corinthians 16:9). That was true in Paul's day and it is true in ours. Wherever God opens an effective door for ministry, there will be opposition from the enemy. I've almost concluded that if you are not getting opposition in your work for God, then you may be doing something wrong! Whenever the world stops criticizing or opposing the church, we know we are no longer a threat and have stopped doing God's work.

The Relief of the Persecution (19:35–41)

Eventually, the "city clerk" (verse 35) was able to calm the crowd and convince them to go home. Remember that Ephesus, like all the region, was part of the Roman Empire. And if there was one thing Rome would not tolerate, it was the disruption of an orderly, peaceful way of life. People were free to live their lives by their beliefs as long as it caused no disruption or disorder. And the political leaders of the town were responsible to Rome to maintain that peace. That's what gave the city clerk incentive to break up the riot—his own reputation and livelihood were at stake.

The clerk told the crowd they were foolish to spend two hours yelling about what everyone knew was true—"That the city of the Ephesians is temple guardian of the great goddess Diana, and of the image which fell down from Zeus" (verse 35). It's obvious that if (according to their mythology) Diana came from heaven, then she is obviously not a god made with hands, as Paul had been teaching (verse 26). This logic made sense to the crowd and quieted them so that they were willing to think better of attacking the Christians and incurring the wrath of Rome.

Further, the clerk explained, if Rome looks into this disturbance, you will have no defense. He pointed out that the Christians were "neither robbers of temples nor blasphemers of [their] goddess" (verse 37). The city courts were available if Demetrius and the silversmiths wanted to bring charges against Paul and the others. If there was to be any prosecution, the clerk said, it would be done lawfully so Ephesus wouldn't be "called in question" by Rome (verse 40). The riot quickly lost its momentum, and the people dispersed.

This statement of G. Campbell Morgan, a great preacher of a previous generation, is worthy of our attention:

Let us be very careful that we do not waste our energy, and miss the meaning of our high calling, by any rejoicing in the patronage of the world. It is by the friction of persecution that the fine gold of character is made to flash and gleam with glory. The church persecuted has always been the church pure, and therefore the church powerful. The church patronized has always been the church in peril, and very often the church paralyzed. I am not afraid of Demetrius. Let him have his meeting of craftsmen, and let them in their unutterable folly shout a lie twenty-five thousand strong. The truth goes quietly on. But when the town clerk begins to take care of us, then God deliver us from the peril.[2]

His point? We do not need the city clerks of this world to protect the church. We are not to cater to the world or seek its favor or protection. If it is God's work, it will have His protection!

Notes:

1. James Montgomery Boice, *Acts: An Expositional Commentary* (Grand Rapids: Baker Books, 1997), 326.

2. G. Campbell Morgan, *The Acts of the Apostles* (New York: Fleming H. Revell Co., 1924), 465.

APPLICATION

1. What did God do through Jesus of Nazareth as reported by Peter in Acts 2:22?

    a. What was God doing by working these miracles? (verse 22)

    b. What should the "men of Israel" have concluded about Jesus, based on these works?

    c. Instead, what did they do? (verse 23)

    d. What was the final attesting miracle God worked through Jesus? (verse 24)

    e. How did the people ultimately respond to these miracles once Peter explained them? (verse 37)

    f. Apply Jesus' teaching in Matthew 13:13–15 to the question of why people then and now can see Jesus' or the apostles' miracles yet not really "see" them for the proofs that they are.

2. In 2 Corinthians 12:12, what does Paul list as the "signs of an apostle?

   a. What do his words suggest about the temporary nature of these signs?

   b. If they are the signs of an apostle specifically, who would we expect not to demonstrate these signs?

3. Read Hebrews 2:3–4.

   a. List the four confirmations God furnished for the message of salvation: (verse 4)

   • _____

   • _____

   • various _____

   • _____ of the Holy Spirit

   b. What warning does the writer give in light of God's confirming evidence? (verse 3)

   c. In what way are believers' spiritual gifts to be a testimony to God's salvation?

d. Describe how your spiritual gift is evidence of your salvation.

4. Describe the miracle God worked through Peter in Acts 5:15 that was similar to the one through Paul in Acts 19:11–12.

   a. What miracle was mediated through Jesus' garments in Mark 6:56 and Luke 8:43–44?

   b. While signs and wonders are not commonplace today, why should you still ask God when you are in need of a miracle? (Mark 9:23; Hebrews 11:6; James 4:2b)

DID YOU KNOW?

As he does more than once in the book of Acts, Luke refers to the Christian movement as "the Way" when describing the events in Ephesus (Acts 19:23). Luke's point is that the opposition in Ephesus was not just toward Paul but toward the impact of the growing Christian movement. There is no clear reference in Scripture as to the origin of the phrase "the Way" to refer to Christianity. Many believe it is rooted in Jesus' words in John 14:6: "I am the way, the truth, and the life." The servant girl in Acts 16:17 uses the phrase in a similar way by referring to "the way of salvation."

THE SECRETS OF PAUL'S SUCCESS

Acts 20:1–38

In this lesson we examine the reasons why people readily followed the apostle Paul.

OUTLINE

The ultimate test of leadership is whether or not anyone is following. Applying that test alone to the apostle Paul means he was a great leader—and his followers have remained. By looking at one snapshot from Paul's life, we can discern nine traits of all great leaders.

I. **Great Leaders Have a Heart for Ministry**
   A. Physically He Embraced Them
   B. Verbally He Exhorted Them

II. **Great Leaders Have a Spirit of Tenacity**

III. **Great Leaders Are Filled with Energy**

IV. **Great Leaders Live Lives of Integrity**

V. **Great Leaders Are Marked by Humility**

VI. **Great Leaders Are Men Under Authority**

VII. **Great Leaders Speak Honestly**

VIII. **Great Leaders Are Given to Generosity**

IX. **Great Leaders Are Followed Passionately**

I became a student of leadership as a young adult—trying to understand what makes great men and women "tick." Any time anyone recommended a biography of, or a book written by, a great leader, I read it.

When I knew God had called me to be a pastor, I continued my study of great leaders, broadening my scope beyond books. And today, I am still fascinated with how God uses people who are totally yielded to Him. And I still have a desire to be that kind of person—and hope you do as well.

I have examined the lives of many, many individuals over the last five decades and have yet to find anyone I love to study more—outside of Jesus himself—than the apostle Paul. I truly believe that no one has influenced life on planet earth more than Paul, with the obvious exception of Jesus Christ.

Going through the book of Acts, we get many glimpses into the heart and soul of Paul; and nowhere do we learn more about him in one setting than in the vignette we will study in this lesson. In Acts 20 we find Paul saying farewell to the elders of the church at Ephesus; it is one of the most moving scenes in the Bible. He somehow knows that he will never see them again, and they weep together at that thought.

We'll look at nine principles of leadership, all of which are found in Paul's interaction with the Ephesian elders. We have a brief record of his leaving Ephesus, going through Macedonia, and then returning to Ephesus for his tearful farewell departure.

GREAT LEADERS HAVE A HEART FOR MINISTRY (20:1–2)

We pick up Paul's story, remembering that a riot had erupted in Ephesus which the city clerk brought to a conclusion after a couple of hours with no harm done to Paul or his coworkers. Paul decided it was time to move on to Macedonia, so he called the brethren together and departed.

Physically He Embraced Them

Paul was a "hugger"—which we need more of among the men in today's church. He embraced the brethren in Ephesus and departed for Macedonia. As he went throughout Macedonia on his way to Greece, he "encouraged [the churches] with many words" (verse 2). Everywhere Paul went, he built up the brethren in the faith.

Verbally He Exhorted Them

Let me quote parts of verses 2 and 20 from *The Message* translation: "He gave constant encouragement, lifting their spirits and charging them with fresh hope . . . . Every truth and encouragement that could have made a difference to you, you got. I taught you out in public and I taught you in your homes."

Paul was a teacher and an encourager. He used his gift of teaching to exhort the brethren to continue in the faith. Everywhere Paul went, he encouraged and exhorted the church to remain strong, to remain committed to truth, and to spread the Gospel. Paul was like a coach who continues to rally his team even when things look bleak. It never occurred to Paul to do anything else. Great leaders don't have to be told to embrace, encourage, and exhort those in the faith—it comes (super-)naturally. They have a heart for ministry.

GREAT LEADERS HAVE A SPIRIT OF TENACITY (20:3-6)

Paul arrived in Greece and stayed there three months (verse 2). Because of a plot against him being formed by the Jews when he was about to sail back to Palestine, he decided to retrace his steps back through Macedonia (verse 3). Paul lived almost his whole Christian life under threat of attack from someone, but it never deterred him. Some examples:

- 9:23 the Jews plotted to kill him.
- 23:12–13 another plot by the Jews to kill him.
- 25:2–3 an ambush was laid for him outside of Jerusalem.

Paul writes in 2 Corinthians 11:23–27 about the myriad kinds of dangers and persecutions he experienced in his life as an apostle, just a portion of which might have derailed a lesser man. But Paul was tenacious—that itself is an understatement. He suffered more in his three decades of apostleship than most people could have endured, yet he never gave up. We have no record anywhere in the New Testament of Paul becoming weak or despairing of his condition.

Great leaders don't quit when things get difficult. Indeed, there is no such thing as an easy leadership role. Leadership, by definition, means enduring difficulty and opposition. But it also means rising early to prepare a Sunday school lesson or spending time in prayer for the work of a committee. There is always a price to pay for leadership.

GREAT LEADERS ARE FILLED WITH ENERGY (20:7–13)

Arriving at Philippi, Paul sailed from there to Troas where he remained for a week in the company of his traveling companions and other believers.

"On the first day of the week" (verse 7), the believers met together "to break bread" and hear a message from Paul who was scheduled to depart the next day. Paul probably began his message around 7:00 or 8:00 p.m., and by midnight he was still going strong.

But then a young man named Eutychus fell down to the ground from a height of three stories and was pronounced dead. The meeting might have been on the flat roof of the building (common in those days) or in a third-story room with Eutychus perched on a window ledge—we don't know the details. Nonetheless, Eutychus fell asleep and crashed on the ground below. Paul immediately went down and fell upon the lad, embracing him, and pronounced him alive— which he was. Never one to let a small matter disrupt his teaching, Paul went back upstairs and continued—"even till daybreak" (verse 11). With the dawn of a new day, Paul departed on foot for Assos.

Paul was a man of incredible strength and energy. After teaching all night, not getting any sleep, he set out the next morning on foot for Assos, a distance of some twenty miles. I believe Paul got that energy from the indwelling Holy Spirit as he functioned in the arena of his spiritual gifts. I recall pastor Bill Hybels saying once that as long as he was ministering in the area of his giftedness, he never lacked for energy. But as soon as he was called on to function in other areas, his energy level quickly dropped.

Because Paul ministered most of the time in his spiritual giftings as a teacher and leader, he had unbounded energy. He could preach until midnight, raise someone from the dead, and continue preaching until dawn! I have marveled through the years at what great leaders have been able to accomplish for God.

GREAT LEADERS LIVE LIVES OF INTEGRITY (20:16)

Paul met up with the rest of his party at Assos and boarded a ship with them, bound for Miletus near Ephesus. Verse 16 tells us that he had originally planned to sail past Ephesus so he would not be delayed in getting to Jerusalem for the celebration of Pentecost (also known as the Feast of Weeks or Feast of Harvest), the great celebration fifty days after Passover.

This is another example of Paul as a Jew seeking to maintain a good conscience toward the Jews he was trying to reach, giving them no opportunity to condemn him for his lack of attention to the traditions of Judaism (Acts 24:16). Because Christ fulfilled all the Jewish feasts, Paul was under no obligation as a Christian to keep the feasts; but he was under an obligation to be a person of integrity toward those whose spiritual understanding was immature.

Integrity means "to integrate; to make one." When you have integrity, you are one person; everything about you is the same; you are the same person to everyone. Paul didn't forget his Jewish kinsmen just because he had become a Christian. He cared for them like he cared for his Christian brethren.

Leaders have integrity—period. They are not perfect, but they are consistent, keeping a clear conscience before God and man. A so-called leader who lacks integrity is not a leader at all.

Great Leaders Are Marked by Humility (20:18–20)

At Miletus, Paul summoned the elders of the church from nearby Ephesus in order to meet one last time with them before sailing for Jerusalem. And he reminds them how he ministered among them "with all humility" (verse 19) when he first came to Ephesus. He "kept back nothing that was helpful, but [proclaimed] it to [them]" (verse 20).

Paul didn't lord it over them. He told them everything he knew; he wanted them to be successful in the Lord. He had no higher goal than that they become mature in Christ. And he was like that everywhere he went (2 Corinthians 1:12). He even worked making tents so that he wouldn't be a financial burden to, or appear to be seeking money from, those he came to serve. He treated the members of the churches he started as his own children (1 Thessalonians 2:7–8, 10-11).

The lives of great leaders emulate the humility and submissiveness of Christ—the one who gave His life in submission to the will of the Father to serve and save the lost.

Great Leaders Are Men Under Authority (20:20, 31–32)

Did you know that everyone answers to someone? And that the test of one's ability to lead is his or her ability to follow?

Paul was a man under authority—he answered directly to God and was happy to do so. He was therefore under the authority of the Word of God. Everything he said and taught was based on the Old Testament and the revelation he had received from God in relation to his conversion, his calling, and his commission.

When it was time for Paul to bid farewell to the Ephesian elders, what did he do? He commended them "to God and to the word of His grace" (verse 32). It is highly instructive that Paul did not commend them to *his* authority. He did not remind them to stay submissive to him and his authority. Instead, he commended them to God, for it is to God that they would ultimately answer. And it was from God that they would ultimately receive their every provision.

GREAT LEADERS SPEAK HONESTLY (20:26-31)

This was not a warm-and-fuzzy meeting. Paul was speaking honestly to the leaders of the Ephesian church; and in doing so, had strong words of warning. He told them that "from among yourselves men will rise up, speaking perverse things, to draw away the disciples after themselves" (verse 30).

What would you have thought if you had been one of the Ephesian leaders? Paul wasn't accusing anyone—he was just being honest, based on something he had seen or knew or felt in his spirit. His warning might have been based on his own experience that wherever the work of God is progressing, there will be those who oppose it or try to capitalize on it for personal gain. His responsibility was to speak honestly to the leaders regardless of the cost. It's something great leaders do not shy away from.

GREAT LEADERS ARE GIVEN TO GENEROSITY (20:33-35)

Paul was not in the ministry to accumulate wealth, nor is any great leader. Paul gave far more to the churches he served than he ever received; and in doing so, he personified the teaching of Jesus that "it is more blessed to give than to receive" (verse 35). Paul supported himself financially so he wouldn't draw down the resources of others (and probably so he would have his own resources with which to help those in need).

I believe any of God's great churches and great leaders are what they are because they are generous. They open their hands when they see a need. Their first response—whether the need is for time, talent, or treasure—is to say "Yes" rather than "No." They are so humbled by all that God has given them that they want to emulate His generosity in their dealings with others.

GREAT LEADERS ARE FOLLOWED PASSIONATELY (20:36–38)

It is obvious that the elders of the Ephesian church respected and loved Paul: "Then they all wept freely, and fell on Paul's neck and kissed him" as he made his departure (verse 37).

One of the ultimate tests of leadership is whether anyone is following or not! And in Paul's case, his leadership was proven by those who followed him—or would have followed him had they been able, as in the case of the Ephesian elders.

Why do we follow the Lord Jesus Christ? It's because He was, and is, a servant-leader. He came to serve, not to be served, and sacrificed himself for our benefit. Paul was followed for the same reason. He had no agenda except to serve Christ by serving others. Anyone with the same agenda will soon be followed—and be a great leader.

May these secrets of Paul's success become the secret of yours and mine.

1. Read Acts 9:15–16.

   a. What was Paul chosen by Christ to do? What two groups were his audience? (verse 15)

   b. In time, how did Paul see his audiences in terms of the Gospel's priority? (Romans 1:16)

   c. What else did Jesus have in store to show Paul? (verse 16)

   d. How did Paul summarize verse 16 several years later? (Acts 14:22)

   e. How did Paul view the sufferings he endured? (1 Thessalonians 3:3)

   f. To what extent was Paul willing to go in obedience to Christ's calling? (Acts 21:13)

   g. How did the Holy Spirit give Paul "reminders" of what Jesus had told him about suffering? (Acts 20:23)

h. How did Paul see his sufferings being connected to Christ?
   (2 Corinthians 1:5)

i. In what way was Paul experiencing the sufferings of Christ?

j. What did he experience in Christ that compensated for
   the sufferings? (2 Corinthians 1:5)

k. On what will the measure of our joy partly depend when
   we ultimately see Christ in His glory? (1 Peter 4:13)

2. Read Acts 26:17–18.

   a. In this version of Paul's testimony, how did he describe his
      mission as given by Jesus? (verse 18)

   b. How did Paul use this wording to describe what happens
      when people are saved? (Colossians 1:13)

   c. How does Satan play into Paul's mission?

d. How does his presence account for the suffering Paul endured?

3. Of all of Paul's leadership traits, which do you admire most— and why?

a. Which of his traits would you most like to develop in your life—and why?

b. In whose life have you seen the most of these traits displayed? To what do you attribute the presence of those traits?

DID YOU KNOW?

The elders of the Ephesian church with whom Paul met on his way to Jerusalem represented one of only two official offices in the early church. Paul had appointed elders in the churches he planted on his first missionary journey (Acts 14:23). Even the founding church in Jerusalem had elders to whom Paul delivered the financial relief gift he had collected in Macedonia (Acts 11:30). Several English terms in the New Testament (depending on translation used) refer to elders: elders (Acts 20:17), shepherds (1 Peter 5:2, NIV), overseers (1 Peter 5:2), and bishops (Philippians 1:1). The other office is that of deacon (Philippians 1:1). Paul eventually laid down qualifications for both (1 Timothy 3).

THE COURAGE OF CONVICTION

Acts 21:1–14

In this lesson we see courage personified in the life of Paul.

OUTLINE

The more challenging the assignment from God, the easier it is to think we may have misunderstood His directions. Our own fears and the discouraging counsel of others can lead us to say "No." Courage is needed when following Christ—courage to obey regardless of the cost.

  I. **Courage That Overcomes the Pressures of Friendship**

 II. **Courage That Overcomes the Prediction of Failure**

III. **Courage That Overcomes the Prophets of Fear**

Has there ever been a time in history when Christians needed more courage than today? The persecution of Christians by the Roman emperors stands out in history as a perilous time, for certain. But in the modern era, Christians are being attacked more than ever—and certainly more than any other religion.

The Israeli political leader David Ben Gurion defined courage like this: "Courage is a special kind of knowledge—the knowledge of how to fear what ought to be feared and how not to fear what ought not to be feared." And the American William Penn once wrote, "Right is right even if everyone is against it, and wrong is wrong even if every one is for it."

The Bible is filled with the record of men and women who were courageous enough to do the will of God. Against all odds and often against the advice of their own friends, they stood for God even if it meant standing against all others.

Noah withstood the criticism of those in his day who didn't believe God was going to judge the earth. He built an ark on dry land at a time when it had never rained—no one even knew what rain was at that time! But Noah persevered in spite of the criticism.

Joshua and Caleb were part of a group of twelve spies who went into Canaan to check out the Promised Land—and they were the only two who had enough courage to believe God would give them victory.

The teenage David was the only Israelite who had the courage to stand against the Philistine giant, Goliath, in the Valley of Elah. His courage resulted in a great victory for the nation over its pagan attackers.

Daniel, when a captive in Babylon, continued praying to God even though he knew it might result in his death. His friends, Shadrach, Meshach, and Abed-Nego refused to bow down to the image of the Babylonian king. Daniel ended up in a lion's den, and his friends were thrown into a fiery furnace. But they were all delivered by God.

While many believers have suffered terribly for their faith through the centuries, statistics are showing that more people are suffering for their faith today than at any time in history. We in the West don't hear as much about this as we should, but martyrdom is not a thing of the past. There is a need for spiritual courage today—and it is likely to increase in the future as we near the second coming of Christ.

As we've seen already, the apostle Paul was a man who needed courage daily—and that need continued as he made his way toward Jerusalem. At this point in Acts, Paul is on the last leg of his third missionary journey, carrying to Jerusalem a large financial gift from the churches in Macedonia and Greece to the beleaguered church in Jerusalem. But his friends tried to dissuade him from going, believing that danger awaited him there.

But Paul was not a man who lacked courage at all, and we will draw three lessons from his experience that can give us the courage we need as believers today.

COURAGE THAT OVERCOMES THE PRESSURES OF FRIENDSHIP (21:1–3)

We last saw Paul bidding a tearful farewell to the elders of the church at Ephesus (Acts 20). The first three verses of Acts 21 recount Paul's voyage from Miletus to Tyre in Syria on the coast of Palestine.

His friends at Ephesus did not want him to leave them. The Greek word for "departed" in verse 1 is a strong word, akin to "tearing away." Paul literally had to resist their efforts to prevent him from leaving. Note Luke's first person use of "we" in verse 1—he was an eyewitness to the bond that was being broken as Paul left the Ephesian elders in Miletus. And yet Paul probably never considered changing his plans. He knew where God wanted Him to go, in spite of the dangers that might exist.

While Luke's travelogue of their journey may seem uneventful, it is another example of the tedious travel that was common in that day. Moving slowly over the water in a boat gave ample time for discussion and reflection on what lay ahead in Jerusalem. But there was no turning back. Indeed, Paul likely relished the daily stops in ports along the way as another opportunity to spread the Gospel.

Many times through the years, I have spoken with Christians who knew what God was calling them to do but couldn't bear to tear themselves away from family, friends, or relationships with which they were involved. It takes courage to serve God—courage that overcomes the pressures that sometimes come from friendships and family. Paul did not give in to those pressures. He pushed ahead to keep his appointment to deliver the relief funds to the Jerusalem church.

COURAGE THAT OVERCOMES THE PREDICTION OF FAILURE (21:4-6)

There is another kind of pressure that arises from (often) well-meaning individuals. They are quick to point out that the course we are on will end in failure. There is always someone who will tell you why what you want to do for God won't work.

Almost everything I've ever tried to do for the Lord has been met with predictions of failure by a few souls. Constructing new buildings, going on radio and television—the bigger the plan, the more people there will be who warn you of impending doom. If you are going to serve God today, you have to do the same thing Paul did: Listen to God, not to men.

Paul arrived at Tyre in Syria and stayed there for seven days. Paul had not planted the church in Tyre. Indeed, it was odd for him to arrive there since the church had been founded during the early days of the persecution against the church of which Paul was a part. Disciples of Jesus had fled Jerusalem and settled in Tyre and other cities; and now, years later, Paul is among them and fellowshipping with them.

Though Paul was only among them seven days, they quickly grew attached to him. The scene at Miletus with the Ephesian elders was repeated in Tyre as Paul and his party prepared to leave. They told Paul "through the Spirit" (verse 4) not to go up to Jerusalem. They feared for his life, given the fact that he had become a follower of Jesus.

The phrase "through the Spirit" doesn't mean Paul disobeyed instruction from the Holy Spirit (though some read it that way). Rather, it means Paul took the words of the believers in Tyre as being a warning through the Spirit of what was going to happen in Jerusalem, but not a prohibition to go. Paul did not yield to the counsel of the Christians in Tyre because he knew what God was calling him to do.

Paul was not a person who disobeyed the command of God, as we saw in Acts 16 when he was forbidden by the Spirit to go into Asia. And when the word came to go to Macedonia, he obeyed "immediately." The Holy Spirit had never said to Paul personally, "Don't go to Jerusalem." In fact, the Holy Spirit had been speaking to him that, wherever he went, "chains and tribulations" awaited him (Acts 20:22–23).

From the very day that Paul was saved on the road to Damascus, suffering had been in his future. The Lord Jesus communicated to him that he was going to suffer "many things" as he went about preaching the Gospel (Acts 9:15–16). So the threat of suffering, even death, was not new for Paul. He was human and did not enjoy suffering. But he had the kind of courage needed to make his way to Jerusalem in spite of the pressure of friends and their predictions of failure.

Paul said in Acts 20:24 that he didn't count his life dear to himself, that he was eager to finish his race with joy—and finish the ministry "[he] received from the Lord Jesus, to testify to the Gospel of the grace of God." Knowing that he had received his ministry from Jesus himself gave added incentive and motivation to see it through regardless of the cost.

Paul had also "purposed in the Spirit" (Acts 19:21) to go to Jerusalem to deliver the relief funds for the church there. Indeed, he said he was "bound in the spirit" (Acts 20:22; "compelled by the Spirit"—NIV) to go. Clearly Paul was not out of the will of God in going to Jerusalem.

Followers of Christ do not lead danger-free lives; we have not been promised any such thing. It requires courage to follow God's direction.

COURAGE THAT OVERCOMES THE PROPHETS OF FEAR (21:7–14)

Paul had overcome the objections of his friends in Ephesus and Tyre and the predictions of his failure. But he probably wasn't ready for a prophet to deliver a message of fear to him concerning his time in Jerusalem. It took an extra measure of courage for Paul to resist the words of a prophet, but he would not be deterred.

When he arrived in Caesarea, he stayed in the home of Philip, the evangelist, one of the original seven deacons chosen to serve the church in Jerusalem. Philip had four unmarried daughters, all of whom were prophetesses, and they were joined by another prophet named Agabus. This prophet had a foreboding message to deliver to Paul—bad things awaited him in Jerusalem.

Agabus was much like one of the Old Testament prophets who used dramatic means for delivering their messages—like Jeremiah, or Nathan who confronted David over his sins. Agabus took Paul's belt and bound his own hands and feet with it, saying, "Thus says the Holy Spirit, 'So shall the Jews at Jerusalem bind the man who owns this belt, and deliver him into the hands of the Gentiles (verse 11).'"

Wow! What would you have thought if it had been your belt, and the message of the prophet had been directed at you? Luke even included himself and the rest of Paul's party among those who were now begging the apostle not to go to Jerusalem. But Paul would have none of their objections: "What do you mean by weeping and breaking my heart? For I am ready not only to be bound, but also to die at Jerusalem for the name of the Lord Jesus" (verse 13).

All those who pleaded with Paul finally recognized the futility of their efforts. They said, "The will of the Lord be done" (verse 14). They finally got in step with Paul and his commitment to do the will of God. They could have saved themselves quite a bit of grief and anxiety if they had taken that step in the beginning.

When Paul got to Jerusalem, as we shall soon see, he experienced all the things that had been prophesied and theorized that would happen. But he was in the will of God, so it didn't matter. That doesn't mean it wasn't painful. But it did mean that it wasn't without value, meaning, or purpose. Paul dialed up his courage to meet the demands that the Gospel placed on his life regardless of what it cost him personally.

We need Paul's kind of courage today—the kind that says, "Regardless of what others think or try to persuade me to do, I'm going to trust God that His plan for me is best—and do it regardless of the consequences."

On April 14, 1521, Martin Luther was on his way to the Diet (ecclesiastical conference) of Worms in Germany. The emperor had forbidden the sale of all of Luther's books and ordered them to be seized. Luther's life was in great danger. His devoted friend, George Spalatin, had sent word to Luther through a special messenger not to come to Worms or he'd be killed. Like Paul, Luther did not listen to his friends. Instead he sent Spalatin the now famous message, "I shall go to Worms, though there were as many devils there as tiles on the roofs."

Later, when Luther was asked to renounce all that he had written in his books and to repudiate them so that he could live, he said, "Since then Your Majesty and your lordships desire a simple reply, I will answer. . . . Unless I am convicted by Scripture and plain reason, I do not accept the authority of popes and councils, for they have contradicted each other. My conscience is captive to the Word of God. I cannot and I will not recant anything, for to go against conscience is neither right nor safe. God help me. Amen."

Martin Luther and Paul were brothers in courage, weren't they? May you and I join them as well. If you are struggling with a decision to follow God's will or to take a stand for Christ, may your courage be unwavering as you obey God regardless of the cost.

1. Read Luke 14:25–33.

   a. What is the importance of the word "great" in verse 25 relative to Jesus' message to the crowds?

   b. How might the size of the crowds have changed after Jesus' message to them?

   c. Explain the word "hate" in verse 26. What is Jesus saying by His use of this strong word?

   d. What does the word "cross" in verse 27 suggest?

   e. How did Paul "hate" (assign a lower priority to the words of) his friends as he headed for Jerusalem?

   f. How do we know the idea of a "cross" was not a threat to Paul? (Acts 21:13)

   g. How does the idea of courage play into the short parables Jesus told in verses 28–32?

   h. How does courage fit into Jesus' words in verse 33? When it comes to courage, what does one have to "give up" for the sake of the Gospel?

   i. In what setting have you been called upon to demonstrate courage for Christ?

j. What kinds of pressure have you experienced not to obey the call of God? How did you respond?

k. At what point after becoming a Christian did someone talk with you about the cost of following Christ, that it would not always be easy, that courage would be required?

l. Why (or why not) do you think this should be part of every disciple's training?

2. Read 2 Timothy 4:6–8, 18.

   a. What was Paul's attitude like at the end of his life? (verse 7)

   b. What did he foresee coming that would make his many sacrifices worthwhile? (verse 8)

   c. How do you reconcile verse 18 with Paul's eventual martyrdom by the Roman emperor?

DID YOU KNOW?

When Paul sailed from Miletus, they arrived first at Cos, then the following day at Rhodes, an island in the Aegean Sea. It's fascinating to think that Paul witnessed one of the seven wonders of the ancient world as he sailed into the harbor at Rhodes: the Colossus of Rhodes. The Colossus was a giant statue of the Greek god Helios, the sun god. It was erected near the beginning of the third century B.C., and stood more than 100 feet tall—probably the highest statue in the ancient world. Tradition says that the legs of the Colossus (in human form) straddled the entrance to the harbor so that ships sailed between them.

THE HUMILITY OF LEADERSHIP

Acts 21:15–26

*In this lesson we discover four aspects of humility
in the life of one man.*

OUTLINE

People who feel proud of their humility obviously don't have it.
Nor do people who debase themselves trying to get it. Someone
has said that humility isn't thinking less of yourself but thinking
of yourself less. That's what Paul did. His thoughts were continually
on God and others.

   I.   **Humility Seeks God's Glory**

  II.   **Humility Surrenders to God's Will**

 III.   **Humility Submits to God's Men**

 IV.   **Humility Sacrifices for God's Church**

OVERVIEW

One of the great stories in the history of the National Football League is the story of Kurt Warner, a man who has demonstrated more humility than any professional athlete I know of.

He was All-State in high school football and tried out at the Green Bay Packers training camp in 1994 after college but was released. Since no other NFL team was interested, Kurt returned home to Cedar Falls, Iowa, and took a job in a grocery store. From All-State to stocking shelves: "It was a difficult and humbling thing, but I think it really helped me to keep things in perspective and not get all caught up in football stuff," he said, reflecting his strong Christian perspective.

He then played in the Arena Football League for three years, then in Europe's equivalent to the NFL where he attracted the attention of the NFL's St. Louis Rams who signed him as a backup to the starting quarterback. When the starter was injured in the 1999 season, Warner was promoted and enjoyed a standout season. He set eighteen NFL records, won the Most Valuable Player award, led the Rams to the first Super Bowl victory, and won the Super Bowl MVP award. He was out of the valley and on top of the mountain.

But there was more. In 2001, Kurt led the NFL in touchdown passes, passing yardage, completions, and completion percentage. He won the league MVP again and led the Rams to the Super Bowl again. In his forty-three NFL starts, his record was 35–8. The records he had accumulated in three seasons would take another long paragraph to list.

In 2002, Kurt started down the other side of the mountain. Due to injuries, he only started six games for which his record was 0–6 while the backup quarterback went 6–0. It got worse in 2003. He suffered a concussion in the season opener and was benched for the rest of the season while his backup led the Rams to the NFC West championship and was selected Pro Bowl MVP.

Rick Reilly, columnist for *Sports Illustrated*, captured Kurt's fate when he wrote, "Destiny kissed him at every turn. And then, for no obvious reason, it was off the mountain of glory, back in the valley of humility for Kurt Warner. . . . But Kurt Warner has accepted his humbling with characteristic humility." Once during the difficult 2003 season when Kurt was the backup quarterback, the starter was struggling. The coach called for Kurt to go in, but he told the coach he thought the starter needed a chance to work through it—which he did, and won the game. Explaining later, Kurt said, "Besides, the Bible says, 'Do unto others as you would have them do unto you.' That's the example I'm trying to set."

With so many sad stories associated with professional sports, it's uplifting to read about a truly humble individual who knows how to put winning and losing in perspective, that it's possible to be successful and humble at the same time.

That's the kind of man the apostle Paul was—great, yet humble. It didn't matter if he was on top of the mountain or in the valley in terms of circumstances, he was always the same: faithful and humble—a giant of the faith. Paul was that rare combination of a leader whom people loved because of his humility and genuineness. There was no arrogance or loftiness about him. He spoke with kings and with the common man in the same way.

He could have been proud and lifted up based on his amazing heritage and training in Judaism. But ever since he was humbled on the road to Damascus by Jesus, he had been emptied of his former religious pride (Philippians 3:7–8). He was filled now with only one mission in life: obedience to the Christ who had confronted him on the way to Damascus, out of gratitude for His forgiveness. In this next installment of our survey of Paul's ministry, we're going to discover four aspects of humility, all of which were manifest in his life.

Paul was on his way to Jerusalem to deliver the relief funds from the churches in Macedonia. When we left him in the previous lesson, he was in Caesarea; and in Acts 21:15, we find him leaving that coastal city and heading "up to Jerusalem"—a distance of about sixty-five miles. Paul's third and final missionary journey reached its conclusion as he arrived in Jerusalem. From Paul's initial days in Jerusalem come four principles of humility.

HUMILITY SEEKS
GOD'S GLORY (21:17–20a)

Paul was warmly received by the leaders of the church in Jerusalem; his exploits for the Gospel were well known. And his stature was undoubtedly raised even further in the church's sight when he arrived with a financial gift for them from the predominantly Gentile churches in Europe.

Paul "told in detail those things which God had done among the Gentiles through his ministry" (verse 19). He told them the same things we have been studying in the book of Acts—a city-by-city account of what had happened in his travels. No doubt this was a fascinating recounting of God's work, given what had happened and Paul's penchant for detail and description.

Luke was careful with his description of Paul's account: "those things which God had done." Paul didn't make himself the hero of the story. Rather, he made sure that the work among the Gentiles was credited to God. Paul never talked about what he had done for God; he talked about what God had done through him. It wasn't Paul who ministered, but Christ ministering in and through him (Galatians 2:20). It's easy to slip into the mindset that we are the ones accomplishing great things for God, but Paul never made that mistake.

If any modern preacher or evangelist had accomplished what Paul saw in his ministry, you can bet there would be a public relations person shouting it from the rooftops. But not Paul. He was not a man who elevated himself in any way. He was content for God to get all the credit (Romans 15:18; 1 Corinthians 15:10; 2 Corinthians 10:7).

At the end of Paul's report, the elders "glorified the Lord" (verse 20)—the perfect response to a report that had glorified God. Humility can be contagious when someone sets the standard for it like Paul did.

HUMILITY SURRENDERS TO GOD'S WILL (21:20b–22)

The elders in Jerusalem transitioned quickly from praise to problems—they were concerned about the reports they had heard about what Paul had been telling the Jews in the regions where he had ministered. It's so easy for us to focus on what we don't like in a situation where wonderful things have been happening.

Here's the background: Estimates are that as many as 50,000 Jews in Judea had converted to Christ while maintaining their zeal for all things Jewish. They were in the process of transitioning from Judaism to Christianity. Many of them continued to observe the Law—not as a means of salvation but out of respect for God and their heritage as Jews.

Some false teachers had crept in and spread lies among the churches, saying Paul was teaching that Jewish believers had to forsake Moses and the Law completely—"that they ought not to circumcise their children nor to walk according to the customs" (verse 21). This was not true, of course, but it is what the Jerusalem elders had been told.

It was not unreasonable for the elders to address this issue—great harm to the church could have been the result of such teaching. While they were appreciative of Paul's work among the Gentiles, they were obviously concerned about what he had allegedly been teaching the Jews.

Paul surrendered himself to the leaders at Jerusalem even though he had been falsely accused. His interest was in the health of God's church, not in his own reputation. It takes humility to be submissive even when you are innocent of wrongdoing.

HUMILITY SUBMITS TO GOD'S MEN (21:23–25)

The elders were concerned that Jewish leaders in the city would hear that Paul was in town and that there might be a major uprising against his presence. So they developed a plan whereby Paul would demonstrate his participation in Jewish customs and take away the evidence by which he might be accused.

The plan: There were four Jewish believers in the church who were ready to end their Nazirite vow (like the vow Paul himself had taken; Acts 18:18). Paul was to accompany them to the temple and participate in the cleaning rituals with them and pay their expenses to have their hair cut and for their sacrificial offerings. By doing so, he would be demonstrating that he was not in opposition to the Law but was fully supportive of it. Because Paul had been living and eating among the Gentiles he had to undergo purification so he could participate at the temple with them.

So Paul agreed—humbled himself before these men who were trying to keep peace in Jerusalem, even though he was innocent of their charges. And he paid, out of his own pocket, the considerable expenses for the other four men who were completing their Nazirite vows. Paul's humility cost him his pride and his money, but he was willing to pay in order to achieve the goal of peace in Jerusalem.

Paul could have debated with the elders and defeated them with ease from a biblical and theological point of view. He could have refused on principle to participate in rituals which he knew were unnecessary from a sanctification perspective. But he didn't. He submitted everything to the elders, to God, and to the greater good in order that no one could accuse him.

HUMILITY SACRIFICES FOR GOD'S CHURCH (21:26)

So the next day, Paul executed the plan, taking the four men with him to complete their vows and offer their sacrifices. There is no indication at all of Paul's resentment or unwillingness to humble himself for the good of the church. He humbled himself before the unbelieving Jewish priests, before the less spiritually mature Christian brethren, and before the elders who had wrongly accused him.

The reason Paul was willing to humble himself in such a fashion is found in 1 Corinthians 9:19–23, one of the greatest passages in the New Testament. We have touched on this passage previously in these lessons, but it cannot be cited too often. It is the place where Paul declares himself to be the "servant of all" that he might win more to Christ. He was willing to become a Jew to win Jews, to be as one under the Law to win those under the Law. He concluded by saying, "I have become all things to all men, that I might by all means save some" (verse 22).

Paul was willing to go to the lowest level necessary to save anyone and everyone. He had absolutely no pride when it came to saving souls. In fact, he believed that he would have been outside the Law of Christ to love his neighbor if he had not put himself under the Law of Moses for the sake of the Jews.

In spite of Paul's efforts, we will see in the next lesson that "Jews from Asia," in Jerusalem for the feast of Pentecost, recognized Paul and stirred up the Jewish population in the city against him (verses 27–28). They accused him of the same things the elders of the church had—of teaching "against the [Jews], the law, and [the temple]" (verse 28).

The rest of the book of Acts is taken up with the results of Paul's encounter with the Jews in Jerusalem. He is arrested, brought before local rulers, and eventually is taken to Rome because he appealed his case to Caesar—his right as a Roman citizen. Paul's case is a textbook example of how doing the right thing does not always lead to blessing, humanly speaking. But it is also an example of how God honors the humble—gives them grace to endure whatever they encounter on their path through this life.

Proverbs 3:34 and James 4:6 say that God opposes the proud but gives grace to the humble. Those verses alone are sufficient reason for us to seek humility in our lives. Who would want to find themselves opposed by God? And who wouldn't rather be the recipient of God's favor and blessing? Humility, or its absence, can make the difference according to the Scriptures.

One contemporary writer has said that humility doesn't mean thinking less of yourself. Rather, it means thinking of yourself less. God doesn't call us to demean ourselves. Instead, He asks us to live a life that honors Him. In so doing, we will find our true place and identity as those whose chief end is to serve Christ and those who need to know Him.

May the humility of the apostle Paul be an example and inspiration to you as you live for Christ.

APPLICATION

1. From Philippians 3:4–6, list the reasons Paul could have used to think highly of himself.

   a. _____ on the eighth day.

   b. from the stock of _____ .

   c. from the tribe of _____ .

   d. a _____ of the _____ .

   e. a legalistic _____ .

   f. zealous about _____ the church.

   g. blameless concerning the _____ .

   h. Even after becoming a Christian, how could Paul have used his background to his own advantage had he desired to do so?

2. Read Philippians 3:7–17.

   a. How did Paul view his impressive Jewish background after becoming a Christian? (verses 7–8)

   b. Why did he discard everything that would have brought him praise from men? (verses 8b–9)

   c. What appeared to be Paul's chief aim in life? On whom was he most focused? (verse 10)

d. What evidence of humility (lack of presumption) do you find in . . .

- verse 11:

- verse 12a:

e Given his "blameless" status as a Pharisee, what would Paul likely have thought about his standing with God? How had that view changed as a Christian?

f. To what extent did Paul view himself as having "arrived" as a spiritual person? (verses 13–14)

g. What prescription for maturity (humility) does Paul give in verse 15?

h. How could verse 17 be interpreted as boasting on Paul's part? Why is it not?

3. Evaluate your own spiritual humility in light of the four evidences cited in this lesson.

a. seeking God's glory

b. surrendering to God's will

c. surrendering to God's leader

d. sacrificing for God's church

4. What was the first step given by God to Israel for receiving His blessing? (2 Chronicles 7:14)

DID YOU KNOW?

The missionary journeys of Paul are usually referred to as his first (Acts 13–14), second (Acts 15:36–18:22), and third (Acts 18:23–21:16) journeys. Paul had every intention of undertaking a fourth journey that would have taken him beyond Rome, westward to Spain (Romans 15:24, 28). There is no evidence in Scripture that he achieved that evangelistic goal, though there is unaccounted time between his first and second Roman imprisonments when he could have. His fourth missionary journey turned out to be unplanned—a journey to Rome to appeal his arrest case to Caesar (Acts 21:17–28:31). He was under house arrest in Rome, released, then rearrested and martyred by Nero around A.D. 66–67.

COURAGE UNDER FIRE

Acts 21:26–22:1

In this lesson we see a demonstration of true courage in the face of overwhelming pressure.

OUTLINE

Some will suggest that courage is proven by becoming as aggressive and unruly as one's attackers. But true courage is illustrated by being able to remain in control of one's senses and spirit in the face of danger. That is the kind of courage Paul manifested when he was attacked.

I. **The Religious Accusers**
   A. Their Accusations
   B. Their Actions

II. **The Righteous Apostle**
   A. His Polite Request
   B. His Proud Reply
   C. His Public Response

C S. Lewis wrote that "courage is not simply one of the virtues, but courage is the form of every virtue at the testing point." That is so very true—and nowhere is courage in the face of testing better personified than in the life of the apostle Paul.

Paul arrived in Jerusalem with the relief funds for the church and delivered them to James and the elders (Acts 24:17; Romans 15:26–28). His first goal completed, his second priority was to help unite the Jewish and Gentile believers into one body. But that plan for the church received a serious blow when Jews from Asia who were in Jerusalem for Pentecost recognized Paul and began stirring up the population of Jerusalem against him. Even though Paul participated with fellow Jews in purification rituals at the temple to show his solidarity with Judaism, he still came under attack.

Paul was not guilty of the charges brought against him by his critics. He never preached against Judaism in terms of its religious expressions, and he did everything he could to become as those under the Law for the sake of winning them to Christ (1 Corinthians 9:20). In spite of his innocence, what we will see in this lesson is the end of Paul's public ministry. Not his ministry, but his public ministry. From this point forward in Acts (except for a brief period in Rome between his first and second imprisonments), Paul is a prisoner of Rome.

Paul had always wanted to go to Rome (Romans 1:10–11; 15:24), but he didn't know he would go as a prisoner. From the moment he was arrested in Jerusalem to his days of incarceration in Rome, Paul was a witness for Christ. It was impossible to be around Paul for any length of time and not learn about God's plan of redemption through Christ. Many in "Caesar's household" (Philippians 4:22) in Rome apparently became Christians. He even wrote four of his letters from prison—Galatians, Philippians, Ephesians, and Philemon.

Though this lesson inaugurates an arduous time in the life of the apostle Paul, it was still a spiritually productive time—a time when true courage is manifested in the face of strenuous testing.

THE RELIGIOUS ACCUSERS (21:26–36)

It's important to understand who was accusing Paul and for what reasons.

Their Accusations (21:26–29)

There were four accusations brought against Paul by his accusers.

1. Denouncing the Jewish People (21:26–28a)

The "Jews from Asia" (verse 27) accused Paul of teaching "against the people" when he was on his missionary journeys in their region—"the people" referring to the Jewish people. These accusations were very similar to the ones brought against Stephen, the first Christian martyr, accusations with which Paul agreed at the time (Acts 6:11–14; 8:1).

They were accusing Paul of being anti-Semitic, an accusation heard during the Nazi rule in Germany before World War II, and an accusation still heard today—a very serious accusation. Why would the Jews in Asia have accused Paul of being against the Jews? It's because, in his preaching, he would tell Jews and Gentiles alike that they could not be saved just by being Jewish, or by keeping the Law, which was true. But they took these words and twisted them to make it seem that Paul had a hatred for Judaism and its adherents.

2. Discrediting the Jewish Law (21:28b)

Next, they accused Paul of being against the Law of Moses. This was an especially serious charge since Jewish tradition held that the giving of the Law of Moses on Mount Sinai took place around the same time as Pentecost was celebrated. So to say that Paul was against the Law of Moses at a time when the giving of the Law was being celebrated would increase the anger of the people toward him.

Of course, Paul was not against the Law. He taught that one could not be saved by keeping the Law but that the Law itself was "holy and just and good" (Romans 7:12).

3. Defaming the Jewish Temple (21:28c)

The Jews accused Paul of teaching against "this place," referring to the temple. When Stephen was martyred, he was accused of being against the temple based on a misunderstanding of Jesus' words about his own body (temple), not the temple in Jerusalem (John 2:19). But Paul had said nothing about the temple. This charge, like the others, was baseless.

4. Defiling the Jewish Temple (21:28d–29)

This accusation is a perfect example of what happens when a mob mentality takes over. Verse 29 tells us that Paul had been seen with Trophimus (Acts 20:4), a Gentile from Ephesus, in Jerusalem. And the Jews just assumed that Paul had taken Trophimus onto the temple grounds and defiled it.

Gentiles were allowed in the Court of the Gentiles on the temple mount, but not into the two inner courts that were reserved for Jews alone. Archaeologists have discovered signs that were posted warning Gentiles not to leave the Court of the Gentiles area. One of them read, "No foreigner is to enter within the forecourt and the balustrade around the sanctuary. Whoever is caught will have himself to blame for his subsequent death."

The fact that Trophimus had not been arrested, even killed, is evidence that he had not violated the temple rules regarding Gentiles. Also, Paul had just gone through the purification rite with the four believers from the Jerusalem church to show his willingness to keep the rules (Acts 21:23 ff.). He would not be so foolish as to negate those efforts by taking a Gentile into a prohibited area of the temple.

Their Actions (21:30–36)

As we have noted earlier, everywhere Paul went there was either a riot or a revival. And in Jerusalem it was a riot—the sixth associated with his ministry in the book of Acts.

1. They Stirred Up the Whole City (21:30a)

Luke uses some graphic terms to describe how the riot started and proceeded: "the Jews . . . stirred up the whole crowd" (verse 27); "all Jerusalem was in an uproar" (verse 31); "because of the violence of the mob" (verse 35). This was a full-scale, dangerous mob intent on killing Paul.

2. They Seized Paul (21:30b)

The crowd seized Paul and dragged him out of the temple precinct and locked the doors so that his blood wouldn't defile the temple grounds (verse 30). They accused Paul of hatred of the Jews and are now exacting a similar hatred toward him. Mobs don't function according to reason, but according to unreasonable passion.

3. They Struck Paul (21:31b–32)

The Jews had begun beating Paul to kill him but stopped when Roman soldiers from the nearby garrison arrived on the scene (verse 32). The Romans had a fortress located on the northwest corner of the temple mount called the Antonia Fortress. They kept a close eye on activities around the temple mount, and it was just such a disruption as the beating of Paul that they were there to prevent.

4. They Sought to Kill Paul (21:31a, 33–36)

The commander of the Roman garrison "immediately took soldiers and centurions" and broke up the mob's attack on Paul. Assuming Paul had done something wrong, he immediately bound Paul in chains and began his inquiry. The crowd was still at a fever pitch; and the commander couldn't get the information he needed, so he commanded that Paul be taken into the barracks for interrogation. The soldiers actually had to pick Paul up and carry him to protect him from the surging, murderous mob. All the time, the crowd was crying, "Away with him!" (verse 36).

Do you recall the prophecy made by Agabus about Paul (Acts 21:11)? He took Paul's belt and bound his own hands and feet and said that Paul would be bound the same way in Jerusalem. And that prophecy was totally accurate. Paul was being carried toward the Roman barracks, bound in chains.

Paul would have certainly died at that moment had the Roman soldiers not intervened. The Jews at least took Stephen outside the city to murder him. But they were so enraged against Paul that they were going to murder him in the city just outside the temple gates.

THE RIGHTEOUS APOSTLE (21:37–40)

Amazingly, Paul was completely in control of his faculties in spite of what was happening to him. He asked for permission to speak to the crowd.

His Polite Request (21:37)

Paul politely asked the commander for permission to speak. Too often, when we are under stress of some kind, we lose all sense of politeness; our spiritual sensibilities seem to leave us. But not Paul. Even in this situation, the fruit of the Spirit is evident in his life. He seems to understand the carnal actions of those who are persecuting him and doesn't hold it against them. He asks only for a chance to speak to them.

His Proud Reply (21:37b–39a)

The commander mistook Paul for an Egyptian false prophet who had raised an army in Jerusalem. The Roman army attacked this terrorist and put down his rebellion, but the prophet himself escaped into the desert. And the commander thought Paul was the Egyptian. That's why he was so surprised when Paul spoke to him in Greek (verse 37).

Paul surprised the Roman commander again by telling him that he was a Roman citizen, "a Jew from Tarsus, in Cilicia, a citizen of no mean city" (verse 39). This put the incident in a new light since Paul had certain rights as a Roman citizen. The commander thought Paul was just a rabble-rouser—the Egyptian, possibly, or just a Jew from Judea. When he discovered that Paul was a Roman citizen, he gave him permission to speak.

His Public Response (21:39b–22:1)

Paul and the soldiers were standing on the stairs leading up to the Antonia Fortress with the mob gathered beneath them. I can't imagine the kind of calm it took for Paul to gather his thoughts and address the very people who, just moments before, had been trying to murder him! Paul was always willing to declare the Gospel regardless of the situation.

When the Roman commander gave Paul permission to speak, the mob fell silent. Paul waited until "there was a great silence" and began to speak to them in Hebrew. He probably actually spoke in Aramaic, which was a dialect of Hebrew and had become the common language of the Jews in the first century. His message to the crowd takes up most of the next chapter of Acts, including his interview with the Roman commander.

You can see now why I quoted C. S. Lewis at the beginning of this lesson that courage is the manifestation of every virtue in a time of testing. Think of all the virtues that were being tested in Paul's life at this moment: love, joy, peace, patience—the full range of the fruit of the Holy Spirit (Galatians 5:22–23). And the evidence of those virtues is seen in the courage Paul demonstrated on the stairs as he prepared to speak to a violent mob of murderers.

Paul is one example of courage, and here's another:

During World War II, Captain Terry Simeral piloted a B-29 Pathfinder plane over enemy targets and dropped a phosphorous smoke bomb to mark the target for approaching bombers. It was his radio operator's responsibility to trigger the bomb and drop it down a tube out the bottom of the plane. On one occasion, the bomb malfunctioned and exploded in the face of the radioman, Sgt. Erwin. It burned his eyes and burned off one ear.

Knowing the burning phosphorous bomb would eat through the metal floor of the plane into the bay beneath and ignite even more incendiary bombs, and knowing the bombers needed that bomb to mark the target, Sgt. Erwin picked up the burning bomb in his bare hands and stumbled toward the cockpit, feeling his way as he went. Captain Simeral had opened a cockpit window to try to clear some of the smoke, and when Sgt. Erwin stumbled into the cockpit he said, "Pardon me, sir," and tossed the bomb out the window. Then he collapsed on the flight deck. For his bravery, he was later awarded the Congressional Medal of Honor while still in a hospital in the Pacific theatre of operations.[1]

Like Paul's courage, the courage of Sgt. Erwin is hard to imagine. It's the kind of courage that emerges in the worst possible times of testing, the kind of courage that responds rather than reacts, the kind of courage that thinks of the good of others more than the good of self.

I'm moved by Paul's example in Acts to always be ready to speak in behalf of the Savior even in times of intense pressure and suffering. May God give us grace to be people of courage for Christ who, like Paul, are able to manifest the power of the Spirit in the face of every test and challenge no matter how severe.

Note:

1. R. Kent Hughes, *Acts: The Church Afire* (Wheaton: Crossway Books, 1996), 181–182.

APPLICATION

1. Read Romans 15:23–33.

   a. Why did Paul want to push on to Spain in his next missionary effort? (verses 23–24a)

   b. Antioch of Syria had been Paul's "sending base" for his first three missionary journeys. How might Rome serve in a similar way in his push west to Spain? (verse 24)

   c. What did Paul need to do first? (verses 25–26)

   d. Explain why the Gentiles in Macedonia "owed" the Jews in Jerusalem their support. (verse 27)

   e. Explain how Paul intended to arrive in Rome, and compare it with how he ultimately arrived there. (verse 29)

   f. Was "blessing" a matter of external circumstances to Paul? Explain. (Philippians 4:12–13)

   g. What did Paul ask the Romans to do for him? (verse 30)

   h. What does "beg" ("urge" in NIV) add to the seriousness of what Paul was feeling about the journey to Jerusalem?

   i. What did he anticipate might happen in Jerusalem? (verse 31a)

   j. Based on what you know of Paul, how did he usually connect "joy" and "the will of God" in his life? (verse 32a)

k. How do we know Paul actually delivered the relief funds to the elders in Jerusalem? (Acts 24:17)

2. Read Romans 9:1–5.

   a. What was the cause of Paul's "great sorrow and continual grief?" (verses 1–2; see 10:1)

   b. What sacrifice would he have made for Israel's salvation? (verse 3)

   c. For what reasons did Paul ascribe "glory" to Israel? (verse 4; see verses 4–5)

   d. How much sense do the allegations of the Jews in Jerusalem against Paul make in light of Paul's heart for his countrymen?

3. What aspect of Paul's life—love, courage, sacrifice— would you most like to emulate in your life?

DID YOU KNOW?

The Antonia Fortress was so named by Herod the Great in honor of Marcus Antonius (Marc Antony), a Roman politician and general. Herod the Great built the Antonia on the northwest corner of the temple mount as a barracks for Roman soldiers who were charged with maintaining order around the temple and in Jerusalem. The Jewish historian, Josephus, described the Antonia as being a large, four-cornered tower, itself having four towers, one on each corner, that allowed clear visibility of the surrounding city. The Antonia was destroyed by the Roman general Titus in 70 A.D. when he laid siege to Jerusalem and the temple mount.

Turning Point
Resources
by Dr. David Jeremiah

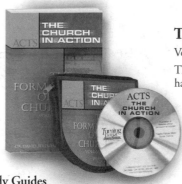

The Church in Action
Volumes 1–4

The post-Pentecost church in Jerusalem has never been equaled for its power, boldness, and effectiveness—and may never be. But that shouldn't stop us from learning and applying its principles. Let *The Church in Action* be your guide to studying the book of Acts.

Study Guides
Volume 1 CIASG1 *(Can - $11/UK - £7)* $10
Volume 2 CIASG2 *(Can - $11/UK - £7)* $10
Volume 3 CIASG3 *(Can - $11/UK - £7)* $10
Volume 4 CIASG4 *(Can - $11/UK - £7)* $10
Study Guide Package CIASGP *(Can - $35/UK - £22)* $32*

Compact Disc Albums
Volume 1 CIAAL1CD (12 CDs) *(Can - $86/UK - £55)* $78
Volume 2 CIAAL2CD (10 CDs) *(Can - $72/UK - £46)* $65
Volume 3 CIAAL3CD (10 CDs) *(Can - $72/UK - £46)* $65
Volume 4 CIAAL4CD (12 CDs) *(Can - $86/UK - £55)* $78
Album Package CIAALPCD (44 CDs) *(Can - $316/UK - £202)* $286

*A 20% Discounted Price

Searching for Heaven on Earth
How to Find What Really Matters in Life

In *Searching for Heaven on Earth*, Dr. David Jeremiah goes verse by verse through Ecclesiastes. He explains Solomon's observations and implementations and shows how they failed—until Solomon's last observation gets it right. Let Solomon be your guide as you learn what doesn't bring meaning in life—and what does.

Hard Cover Book SFHHBK *(Can - $28/UK - £13)* $22
Journal SFHJ *(Can - $16.25/UK - £7.65)* $13
Study Guide SFHSG *(Can - $11/UK - £7)* $10
Compact Disc Album SFHALCD (12 CDs) *(Can - $86/UK - £55)* $78

ORDER 1-800-947-1993